WITHDRAWN

Hidden in Plain Sight

Hidden in Plain Sight

How to Create Extraordinary Products for Tomorrow's Customers

Jan Chipchase
with Simon Steinhardt

HARPER
BUSINESS

An Imprint of HarperCollins*Publishers*
www.harpercollins.com

Grateful acknowledgment is made for permission to reproduce from the following: Excerpt from *Portfolios of the Poor* by Daryl Collins, Jonathan Morduch, Stuart Rutherford, and Orlanda Ruthven. Copyright © 2010 by Princeton University Press. All rights reserved. Reprinted with permission.

FIRST EDITION

Designed by Janet M. Evans

Library of Congress Cataloging-in-Publication Data
  Chipchase, Jan.
    Hidden in plain sight : how to create extraordinary products for tomorrow's customers / Jan Chipchase and Simon Steinhardt.— First edition.
        p.   cm.
      ISBN 978-0-06-212569-9
      1. Marketing research. 2. New products. 3. Consumer behavior. I. Steinhardt, Simon. II. Title.
      HF5415.2.C46 2013
      658.5'75—dc23
                                2013003930

13 14 15 16 17   OV/RRD   10 9 8 7 6 5 4 3 2 1

Contents

Hidden in Plain Sight

Introduction

You might find my line of work exotic, adventurous, or even a little eccentric, but ultimately I'm just trying to figure out what makes people tick.

A large part of my job is to spot and decode the little things that most people take for granted—something that many of the world's most distinguished companies will pay handsomely to understand. The work might have me attending Sunday church services in Utah; walking the aisles of a big-box do-it-yourself store in the Tokyo suburbs; or rising at the crack of dawn to document how a suburban street wakes up and reveals itself to the world.

Other times I'm looking to the extremes and to the future, engaging in activities that help me to better understand the outliers that may someday become mainstream behaviors: borrowing money from loan sharks in Malaysia; talking my way out of police detention in a remote Chinese desert; riding two-up on a motorbike through rush-hour Kampala; or walking through some of the more crime-ridden streets of Rio with pockets stuffed full of cash.

Risk, like most things, is relative.

Personally, I think joining a woman on a shoe-shopping expedition in Shanghai is more dangerous than trying to figure out the going rate for a used Kalashnikov in Kabul. Any sign of a camera in the shoe shop and you'll be approached by the security staff, who'll assume you're a rival trying to reverse-engineer their store. In Kabul, no one worries about a camera-wielding foreigner; the guns are already assumed to be elegant copies available for sale to all comers.

Yes, my job does have its charms. After a day spent evading guards and sleeping atop a Mayan temple, I've woken to a stunning dawn above the jungle foliage. I've strapped my bicycle to the top of a coconut boat and sailed gingerly up the Mosquito Coast. When you love what you do and understand how it might be of value to your well-paying clients, the line between work and play becomes deliberately hazy.

Usually I have a camera with me. These days it's a chunky, stripped-down Canon EOS 5D Mark II that has more than earned its high sticker cost, capturing hundreds of thousands of moments for posterity; for analysis; and for teammates, clients, research participants, and others to see. I'm not a professional photographer, but you could say I'm a professional observer of the ordinary. In most of the places I visit, I spend a lot of time looking at ordinary people using ordinary objects to do ordinary things: making a call on a mobile phone, retrieving cash or a credit card from a wallet, filling up a gas tank from a pump. What I see in these ordinary situations—hidden in plain sight from most others—may be the spark that opens up untapped global markets for my clients. I try to spot opportunities that give clients distinct competitive advantages, whether they're delivering the most low-tech bar of soap or the most high-tech wireless network. Some of these opportunities are driven by profit motive; others a combination of profit and a desire to help address some of the world's most pressing social issues: health care, education, and poverty, to name a few.

What I see in all of these situations are the things most of us take for granted: the motivations that drive human behavior. "Why," I'm constantly asking, "are they doing that? And why in that particular way?"

The Case for Why

If you want to understand people, you have to understand how people function in the wild, in their natural settings, in a world of chaos and gray areas, a world with consequences, a world that's constantly changing.

I have a great deal of respect for academic researchers who are able to conduct scientifically rigorous experiments with a close eye on how tweaking one or more variables will impact the outcome. Their findings provide a strong foundation for my work (as you'll see throughout this book). Through the happy accident of a past life as a poor academic, I've come to appreciate nontraditional ways of finding an audience, and have found that ultimately it's not possible to shoehorn the essence of life into dry academic journal articles.

My work—as well as this book—is about scratching beneath the surface to find reality in bits and pieces, and to use those bits and pieces to see the world in a richer, more textured way. In turn, we can use that newfound perspective to forge better relationships, solve some very tricky problems, make more useful and desirable things, and generally better appreciate the world for what it is.

From a business perspective, there are 7 billion* (and counting) reasons that necessitate a shift in perspective: the ability to zoom in on finite details—a train station in Tokyo, a coffee shop in Beirut, a schoolteacher's apartment in Kabul—in order to get a fix on the big picture. Thanks to the Internet and modern logistics and supply chains, almost anyone in the world could be your customer (or your customer's customer), but you'll forfeit those opportunities if you don't make the effort to figure out who they are, and the nuances of what they want and why.

Of course, not everyone in the world wants the same things, and certainly not everyone can afford the same things, but you'd be surprised at what people can manage—and what they desire—even with meager resources. Roughly 80 percent of the world lives on fewer than $10 a day,† yet more than half the global populace owns a mobile phone.

Those numbers speak to the purchasing power of the developing world, but they also illustrate how a disruptively compelling technology like the mobile phone can reshape the global market. You'll hear me come back to the mobile phone frequently throughout this book, partly because a significant chunk of my career has been spent working in the communications industry. Primarily, though, it's because the mobile phone is the most visi-

---

* Global population was 7,045,832,082 as of October 15, 2012, according to the U.S. Census Bureau's International Database.

† Based on 2005 data for $USD Purchasing Power Parity (PPP), according to the 2008 World Bank Development Indicators report.

ble manifestation of one of the biggest disruptors in recent times—personal and convenient connectivity. It may no longer seem radical, but the ability to reach into one's pocket and retrieve a device that can then reach out to just about anyone, anywhere, anytime, immediately, and with the choice to do so either publicly or privately, has reshaped human interaction across the globe.

When you flick a switch and the room lights up, you're not thinking about all of the different elements that go into making that work: the wiring in the home; the molds used to make the lampshade; the lightbulb; the experimentation and eventual standardization that made it feasible to wire up whole towns; how to generate, store, and transfer electricity. In that previously darkened room there are more important things at stake than understanding how it all hangs together, for example, things like trying not to trip over the coffee table. When you flick that switch, "technology" doesn't get a second thought.

And it shouldn't, as long as it's designed well enough to "just work." While there's a vibrant global technology scene, only a small subset of society has the tolerance to put up with things considered by the mainstream to be not quite there yet. From the consumer's perspective, and for most goods, when the current standard appears to be good enough, why waste the time trying something new that may or may not work?

It's worth taking a step back here to talk about what I mean by "technology." At various points in my career, including notably during my stint as a concept design scientist at a Tokyo research lab, I've been deeply immersed in both cutting-edge technology and technologists—people whose job was to push the boundaries of anything from batteries to fuel cells, new kinds of displays to new forms of wireless connectivity. I've also worked for many of the world's leading technology and engineering companies, been given carte blanche to buy the latest tech, worked out of some of the most high-tech cities in the world (Tokyo, Seoul, San Francisco, among others), and been able to travel to early-adopting communities where they had already rolled out new technology that the rest of the world had yet to see in place. To do my job right requires a baseline understanding of where technology is at and where it is heading.

When I think of "technology," though, I don't just mean electronics or the services that sit around them. My definition of "technology" is far broader, from initial awareness and the drivers for adoption; consumer literacy around a technology's perceived value, and the accuracy of those assumptions; how that value plays out in the way it's used in the real world; and so on. As you'll see later in this book, I'm also interested in how our assumptions around a technology's use change once it's introduced. Technology isn't restricted to things with batteries, displays, connectivity, or wires, even though more and more objects now possess these features. At various points in history the iron skillet, the mechanical wristwatch, and the pencil were considered instruments of modern technology, until that point when people started to take for granted their properties, the consistency of their manufacture, and the permanence of their existence, at which point they started to fade into the background.

Every new technology put out on the market is introduced with assertions and assumptions about how it will be used, but it's only through actual experience that "use" is defined, shaped by any number of factors including context, personality, motivation, and income. Some technologies reach a milestone in their evolution that accelerates or spurs new kinds of use, new reasons for adoption. For email or chat, that spur might be network effects where the presence of more people on the network provides a greater utility, which pulls even more people onto the network. For a technological object like a phone, it might be a reduction in size, supporting portability and the range of contexts in which it becomes convenient to carry that object. For yet another it could be battery life, robustness against breakage, or price. New users, new contexts, and new ways of using all lead to new patterns of behavior, which in turn change our expectation of what a technology is and could be.

Some companies are disposed to putting technology out there in its rawest form to see how the market (or a subset of the market, such as early adopters) will react. Countries such as China, Japan, and South Korea—often those that are close to the manufacturing process—tend to see more experimentation in the marketplace, since the cost of putting it out and refining the design later is arguably lower. (My observation regarding electronics manufacturing in Japan has been that many products are designed for the Japanese market first and only by version three are they mature enough for the less forgiving international market.) Companies with existing brands to protect tend to be more conservative about what they put on the market, not wishing to upset their existing cash cows.

The assumption that technologies fade into the background never to be heard again is largely a Western one. The fade of technology is smoother when we aren't reminded that it's there: if it largely works as expected; if when it breaks it's either replaced as a whole rather than in parts (think toaster) or in a modular fashion that limits what we see of the underlying technology (think inkjet cartridge); or if it includes a business model that limits how much we need to think about the ongoing cost of use (think subscriptions). But in most parts of the world, the underlying infrastructure is much less reliable, more likely to be used near capacity, and there are more highly resource-constrained consumers with business models that encourage careful reflection on the costs of use at the time of use.

The net result is that consumers are reminded of the underlying technologies and they live in a society that retains a higher volume of literacy. Just as technology is not adopted evenly across the board, it does not fade evenly either. I've spent years tracking the evolution of repair cultures around the world from Afghanistan to India, Nigeria to Indonesia, and how people acquire the literacy, skills, and awareness to repair even the most complex technologies. This is not to say that the desire to understand technology is especially great there, but rather that the *necessity* to understand technology, to appreciate the different ways it might be used, is greater, because at a base level it's a useful skill for survival. As I'll show later on, this high level of awareness, literacy, and drive to understand the underlying properties of technology can lead to different usage patterns than the original designer(s) expected (if there was a designer at all) and lead to significant new business opportunities.

I traveled to Uganda in 2006 to better understand the extent to which people were happy sharing their communication tools (and mobile phones in particular) versus the desire to own their own. For the client, the answer would impact whether they would redesign their existing product or produce hundreds of millions more of the products they had on the market. As part of the project I looked into a new service called Village Phone, which was bringing mobile connectivity to rural villages that were, at the time, at the edge of the cellular grid (today almost all of these places are blanketed by cellular coverage, such is the pace of change). The program was jointly run by Grameen Foundation USA, partnering with local microfinance organizations, and MTN (the regional mobile telecom provider), with handset support from Nokia and Samsung. The program was interesting enough, but the thing that surprised me most was witnessing a practice that was far ahead of anything I'd seen elsewhere in the world, despite there being no design process, and no formal service offering: one of the first instances of mobile banking.

Consider what happened in Kampala, Uganda's capital, a bustling urban center with a population of more than 1.4 million. Like many cities, it draws waves of migrants from the nation's countryside with the promise of jobs. Those migrants often leave families behind in their villages, a separation made even more difficult by the lack of affordable communication infrastructure in many rural areas. The Village Phone program provided the technology—a phone, a car battery (a common power source in places that are off the electrical grid), and a powerful TV-like antenna to plug into the phone that could pick up a cellular signal from up to thirty kilometers away (the default is closer to twenty kilometers).

The microfinance organization provided a loan to an entrepreneur (usually female) within a given village who could then charge fellow villagers to use the phone. It's not surprising that supplying connectivity to places that didn't previously have it is a compelling proposition, and that people would be willing to pay for the convenience. However, the organizations behind Village Phone, and everyone else operating in that space, were blind to the potential peripheral benefits that such connectivity could provide. They didn't see that they had a tool that could help people overcome pressing everyday problems, because they didn't bother to look into what those problems were—such as the need to transfer money across great distances.

Let's say Akiki wants to send money from Kampala to his wife, Masani, in their village. In the old days, there were two ways he could do this. One way involved Akiki opening a bank account (if he had the necessary documentation and was considered a viable customer), depositing money into it, sending word back to the village that there was money in the account, and then having Masani take a long taxi ride to the nearest bank to retrieve the money. Beyond the sheer inconvenience and cost of the taxi, delays in the banks' processing systems meant that the money wasn't always there when the villager arrived. The banks also made it difficult to transfer small sums of money, so Masani would have to wait while Akiki saved up enough to make a reasonable deposit. The other way was for Akiki to recruit a bus driver heading to his village to deliver cash to Masani, but there were limited assurances that the driver would deliver it to the right person, or would be trustworthy. Not exactly what you'd call a secure transaction.

It was during our research in rural Uganda in villages beyond the asphalt streets that we repeatedly came across people who talked of *sente*, of sending money without any access to formal money transfer services, but rather by using a workaround through the existing communications business model and infrastructure. Instead of sending cash directly to Masani, Akiki would use that money to buy mobile phone airtime credit from one of the many vendors that lined Kampala's Nakasero Market, only he wouldn't redeem the credit for himself (in fact, back in 2006 Akiki most likely wouldn't own a phone).* Instead, he would call the phone kiosk operator back in the village and give her the code to redeem the airtime, which she could then charge villagers to use. In turn, the kiosk operator would pay out the cash equivalent of that airtime, minus a transaction commission of 20 to 30 percent, to Masani. No banks, no buses, no taxis. Problem solved.

No one knows the first person who tried the informal sente process. There was no ribbon-cutting ceremony, no glowing write-up in the press, no commemorative plaque, and no practical trace of that first transaction. It was simply someone trying to figure out how to save time and effort using the resources at their disposal. And the spread of the practice happened quickly, as those kiosks were often social hubs through which information flowed, and the knowledge of what worked for one customer would rapidly be offered to another. For all the effort by organizations from Grameen Foundation to the largest mobile operators and mobile phone manufacturers, it's difficult to imagine designing something so attuned to local conditions, sensibilities, and tastes.

---

* As of 2006, the rate of mobile phone ownership in Uganda was 4 percent, while the rate of usage was 80 percent.

Informal sente was far from perfect: there was no automated receipt mechanism (the receiver would need to call the sender back confirming that the money arrived); there were occasional mix-ups, with money delivered to the wrong person with the same name; there might be squabbles about the amount of commission; and sometimes the kiosk operator wasn't able to cash out all the airtime in one go. While the existing behavior demonstrated demand, these visible shortcomings suggested an opportunity for a formal, designed service.

Around this time in neighboring Kenya, Nick Hughes and Susie Lonie of Vodafone UK, with seed funding from the United Kingdom's Department for International Development, were running a trial to explore more efficient microfinance repayments. As the trial progressed, it became apparent from interactions with customers that there was scope for a commercial person-to-person money transfer service. Upon launch in 2007, they expected to attract 200,000 customers in the first year; they got that many within the first month. Most of these prepay customers were already topping up their phones with airtime; some were practicing the local variant of sente. Today, Kenya's M-Pesa is considered one of the most successful mobile banking services in the world. And Uganda Telecom has since launched their formal mobile wallet offering, M-Sente.

The informal practices around airtime transfers and converting airtime to currency played an important role in this growth: building literacy around mobile use; generating trust in the process of transferring abstract things (airtime, money); making it easier to identify areas for improvement; and ultimately priming expectations as to what could be.

There are many ways to explore current behaviors and to understand how this insight can be used as a foundation to extrapolate the future. One method is to find *emergent behaviors*, essentially things that people have only recently started doing and that might, if the conditions are right, become widespread. Emergent behaviors can be triggered by cultural memes—like a gesture triggered by an Olympic winner on the podium, natural disasters that overcome entrenched social norms, or the introduction of a business model and subsequent ways to skirt it, such as mobile phone customers who call each other and hang up immediately as a way of making contact without being charged for airtime usage.

One of the techniques that can reveal or amplify these behaviors is to trigger situations that nudge people toward new actions. Another, arguably more ethical version of the same thing is to find people who are already in extreme (at least from the perspective of the mainstream) situations—people whose situation or context pushes them to make the most of what is currently available regardless of existing social or legal norms. Call it innovation by necessity. These people are often called "extreme" or "lead users."

Johor Baharu is a shabby border town on the Malaysian side of the Singapore-Malaysia border known for economic tourists looking to shave a few cents off the price of their gasoline, migrant workers passing through to work in the pristine city, and a wide spectrum of nightlife. It also appears to have a gambling problem. One of the features of many residential streets is a plethora of high-interest, short-term loan advertisements zip-tied to street signs, and the detritus of past advertisements points to a highly competitive marketplace for these loan services.

I was in Johor Baharu with a team exploring attitudes and practices around money for a client wishing to introduce new global mobile money services, and this outlier piqued our interest: why would anyone borrow money *at 100 percent interest for two days*? It seemed irrational, but if it happened then there must have been a rationale. To explore this, we could have interviewed these extreme or lead users, but there was another, more empathic way that could literally put the researcher into the borrower's shoes: we decided to take out one of these loans ourselves, and in the process learned the ins and outs of extreme finance. Aside from physical collateral (they held on to one of our cameras until the loan was repaid), the loan shark's risk mitigation strategy included driving by where we lived, photocopying the identification card of my female assistant Anita, and taking her photo with his camera phone. This last act was a signal that, ultimately, *she* was the collateral.

Most of you reading this will assume without a doubt that you are the sole owner of your identity, and that although it can be stolen by fraudsters, you can't simply sign it away. But it turns out there are many situations in the world where, for people who have very little else, individual identity (and the reputation that comes with it) is the one piece of collateral they have, and in effect they are handing it over to other people to control. In the case of borrowers in Johor Baharu who don't repay their loans on time, their homes are first daubed with red paint, and if payment is still not forthcoming their photos are posted up on boards around their community with the caption "Do not give

this person a loan," in an effort to protect the lender's investment by shaming the borrower's family into paying. The threat
of these measures turns out to be a particularly prickly form of
motivation for timely repayment, as it seems that the label of
"money borrower" is so highly disgraceful in Malaysian culture
that it actually fuels the loan shark system. People would rather
pay outrageous interest rates than face the indignity of reaching
out to family members. Stigma can't be measured in dollars and
ringgit, but it's an economic factor just the same.

This sort of "contrasting rationality," whereby differences in
cultural values lead to divergent decision-making processes, can
come into play in just about any cross-cultural interaction,
which makes it incredibly important to cultivate a sixth sense:
the sense of "why."

Why haven't lower-middle-class Indians embraced the Tata
Nano, a car that was designed for their budgets with a starting
price of about $2,900? Why do they instead go for the Maruti
Suzuki Alto, which costs more than twice as much? The common perception is that people with low incomes will consume
the goods and services that fit their meager budgets, which is to
say cheap crap. That's just not true. If you used your sense of
"why" to uncover the truth about what low-income people want
by talking to the people who know best—those people
themselves—you'd find that they are in fact some of the world's
toughest customers. Because they have to make every rupee
count, they can least afford to buy poorly designed products.
Even with $2,900 at hand, they can't bear the cost of spending it
on a car that is rumored to spontaneously catch fire, leaving
them with no car and no means to replace it.

The Nano still has tremendous potential, since a $2,900 car—a functional one—can be a disruptive force of change in the marketplace, just as a $100 laptop or a $20 mobile phone can. These objects can be powerful tools in people's everyday lives, *if* they actually help people overcome the fundamental obstacles they face—transportation, education, communication, and so on—*and* are designed as desirable objects that convey a positive image of their owners. Businesses, nonprofits, governments, and scientists aiming to provide these kinds of solutions can only do so with a textured, nuanced understanding of the people they aim to serve. Why do people live the way they do? How do they cope with the costs of living when paid work is scarce? What motivates their decisions at any particular turn?

Off the Beaten Path

There's a particular type of traveler that many of us know: the tourist who never strays from the well-worn path of landmarks and tourist traps, who only sees the side of another culture that has been handpicked for people like him, and returns home with a very predictable—and incomplete—experience. Then there are those who like to explore, to get lost on purpose and let the unexpected find them. Unlike the first form of travel, those who allow themselves to get lost in the new environment have fewer guarantees and a greater risk of disappointment (and mugging), but there is also an infinitely greater chance of new and unique experiences that will prompt new ideas and points of view.

Just as travelers can easily fall into tourist traps in the name of efficiency and expectations, even the most highly trained and skilled ethnographic researchers can get bogged down through rote practice.

At the risk of gross oversimplification, the typical international design research study goes something like this: the team jets into a new locale, checks into a corporate hotel, syncs with a recruiting agency, and bounces around the city in taxis to conduct contextual interviews, returning to the corporate hotel at the end of the day enthused and physically and mentally spent. The team's taste of local flavor tends to be incidental—a snatched meal, half an hour to shop for essentials, a late night out on the town once the interview notes are written up. Repeat this process for a couple more cities, and by the time they get together to synthesize their findings the team has worn out its enthusiasm. Are they informed? Kinda. Are they inspired? Depends.

But there's a better way to do it.

It starts with the scouting process, looking for the neighborhoods where the team can get a sense of the denizens' everyday lives. That means fanning out from the city center, looking for residential areas with a mixture of industry and local commerce. Rather than corporate hotels, I try to have our team stay together in a house:* usually a rental property, but occasionally with a host family. It's cheaper than a hotel, we get to embed ourselves in the culture, and it brings the team closer together.

------

* When the project goal includes design we often call these "pop-up studios," with the setup mimicking much of the larger home-base studio setup, albeit with adjacent living accommodation.

Nothing says camaraderie like taking a one-minute shower to save some hot water for your five fellow team members.

Other researchers tend to hire their local assistants through an employment agency that can provide them with experienced help. I prefer to go through the local university and hire students—not just any students but smart, socially active ones. They take us to inspirational pockets of the city for our daily team debriefs, give us access to their social networks, and attune us to the nuances of local culture. A fresh set of eyes on a project means a fresh perspective and new ideas on the table. Whenever possible I try to make room for the students to stay with the rest of the team.

Instead of guides and translators, I usually try to hook up with fixers, the secret weapons of international journalism. They have some of the strongest local connections and understand the ethnographic hustler's social tap dance: controlling interactions just enough to get to the questions, then letting the interviewee control things from there so they can provide meaningful answers.

When we arrive in country, we don't have much time to get acclimated, but whatever time we can manage tends to be the most valuable time we have. That's when we break out our secret weapons—or more likely, head down to the nearest bicycle shop to pick them up.

Cruising through the city on bikes doesn't feel like work, but it gives us a chance to rapidly engage with the environment on a human level. We get to experience the flow and the tempo and cadence of the city. Most important, it puts us on the same plane of urban life as the other thousands or millions who occupy the city.

One of my favorite ways to do this early on in the study, and one of simplest, is to wake up with the city. Gather the team before dawn, find an appropriate neighborhood, then cruise around together while the shopkeepers are lifting their shutters, as newspapers hit the pavement and locals step out for their morning constitutionals. The morning rush for essentials—from coffee or chai to fresh pastries to rice porridge—is a ritual virtually everywhere, making it ripe for cross-cultural comparisons. If there's a long line, all the better: our job, after all, is to strike up conversations.

Some conversations end up being more revealing than others, and those are the ones we seek out. The key is to find the spaces that are most conducive: where people hang out, talk openly, and feel safe enough to give a stranger the time of day—because we'll routinely approach them and ask for it. Barbershops can be particularly promising, so I'll go for a shave (sometimes twice a day) and chat up whoever's around. If we can string out the conversation long enough to do an interview for the study, great; if the participants feel comfortable inviting us into their homes to do the interview, even better.

We spend a fair amount of effort making sense of all this data at every step of the process, as you'll see in the chapter that follows, and by the end of our time in a city the live-work space feels like Mission Control, with every inch of wall space covered in maps of the city, participants' profiles, and hundreds if not thousands of observations, quotes, and insights. In and among it all are the gems that can lead to the Next Big Thing.

A Habit of Mind

People starting out in their own careers* often ask me how I ended up with a dream job. My job is incredibly fulfilling, but in ways many people aren't able to appreciate. I haven't "ended up" anywhere. It's a journey, and I'm still figuring out how to make sense of it, and how to balance it with family, life, love, and ultimately delivering value to clients.

Many things have shaped this journey, including, yes, trips to both near and far-flung corners of the world; long road trips laid the groundwork for cultural understanding and insight, even if at the time they might have felt more like travel for pleasure than work. Two realizations in particular have shaped my thinking on how to make the most of life, and have had an impact on how I "ended up" in this career.

The first is that there are probably only a handful of big decisions that need to be made in a lifetime, and everything, no matter how important and all-consuming it seems at the time, will fade. The question is, of course, whether we are able to recognize these moments for what they are at the time, and put the energy into achieving the optimal outcome. Perspective, gained from thoughtful reflection on our own experiences as well as others', frees us up to enjoy the nuances of the ride. It also speaks to how we evolve as people and how what seems insurmountable now can become just another thing you are able to do.

---

* And seasoned journalists. For some reason journalists think that I have their job, but with a bigger expense account and without the deadlines.

One of these life decisions took me and my then-girlfriend/ now-wife from the United Kingdom to Tokyo with little money, no job, and very limited Japanese language skills, but an intense desire to learn from a country that at that time was at the cutting edge of combining physical and digital design. If you're looking to get ahead in your own field, you need to think about where you need to be situated to be able to learn the most, and ask yourself why aren't you there already. For me, at that point in my career, that place was Tokyo.

Every time I stepped out the door of our apartment I was able to experience or learn something new, and almost a decade later, up until the day we flew out to our next home, Tokyo was still revealing itself. Over time, this principle of being "based out of" somewhere interesting has morphed with my career, where the benefits of spending more time in one particular place gives a different and deeper understanding, even if it sometimes comes with a little pain. Let me explain: It's one thing to be a paid observer, and to structure visits to places in ways that go below the surface, but these visits are just that—inherently limited in what they reveal. The experiences to be appreciated more deeply come when the honeymoon period wears off, when you're faced with dealing with what everyone else deals with: paying bills, buying groceries, petty theft, visiting the doctor, balancing budgets-work-life-friendships, and dealing with the worst that a commute can throw at you. That's when the understanding of a city really kicks in.

Over the years I've been based out of cities on three continents, with each move triggered by life and career-stage and an intense appreciation of what being there does and doesn't mean.

The desire to better understand the planet and its inhabitants will no doubt lead us onto the next.

The second realization relates to the role of failure and goes back to when I was at school in the coastal resort town of Brighton, England. I was an average student and mostly appreciated school, but I rarely applied myself academically—there was simply too much else to enjoy. It should have come as no surprise that I failed my university entrance exams, not just in terms of falling short of my preferred universities, but actually not getting into any university. Academically, I was that bad. Although they never talked about it in those terms, it definitely hurt my parents, who had invested so much in providing the opportunity that university affords.

With the support of my family, we enacted a backup plan that had me retake exams and apply for university a year later. But it was during the time between failure, retaking exams, and scraping into university that the seeds to my career were planted. I moved in for a while with relatives in Berlin, and it was there, living for the first time in another country, that I truly began to appreciate that the world wasn't centered around England, as I had always imagined.* The simple act of standing in another geographic location and looking at a map of a city, country, or the planet helps underline that we're not "there" anymore but are now "here." It forces into motion a whole string of mental

---

* One of my tests for understanding people's cultural standpoints, and where they center themselves in the world, is to have them quickly draw a map of the globe. It is often this worldview that they carry with themselves for the rest of their life.

processes that ultimately helps us shape what we want out of life: where to live; what values to live by; the importance of our existing social circle over exposure to the new; how to reinvent; and the list goes on. Maps are powerful in many ways, not least in that they allow us to reimagine the world and our place within it.

In Plain Sight

Over the course of this book, I'll show you how to look at ordinary human activities in a whole new light, so that you too can crack the social code for the sake of insight, inspiration, and quite possibly a career.

We'll start our journey with a look at how to make sense of any behavior by exploring what I like to call thresholds—those transitional points between doing and "don't-ing." We'll also examine how the objects we buy and carry shape and represent who we are in the world, how we show up and show off, and how, when, and why we choose to adopt them. We'll examine commonalities and anomalies: the link between a $20,000 mobile phone and a $1 bit of wire made to imitate orthodontic braces, and what the use of hybrid corn seed in Iowa can teach us about the popularity of BlackBerry in Nigeria.

Our focus will span from personal space and technologies into the public space: how we navigate the social sphere, and what objects and technologies light our paths. For instance, I'll show you how reading signs ("don't drink this water" or "no dogs allowed"), posters, and billboards can tell you more about a local culture—why people do certain things but not others—than any travel guide. We'll explore how trust is signaled between businesses and consumers, why every context has its own "trust ecosystem," and how it affects the products and services sold within those ecosystems. We'll examine what the things people carry (mobile phones, keys, money, and other survival instruments) tell us about life on the go, what happens when those things become digital and intangible, and how you can decode "carrying behaviors" today in order to create the mobile products and services of the future.

Finally, we'll examine the ways people with limited resources devise ingenious solutions to often-complex problems, and what the designers and developers of even the most high-tech products can learn from the world's poorest consumers. I'll show you how a bottle of gasoline, a brick, and a hose on a dusty backstreet in Ho Chi Minh City comprise the purest essence of a service delivered elsewhere by some of the world's wealthiest corporations. We'll see what happens when messy problems lead to even messier solutions. Consider, for instance, why illiterate people would rather fumble with a standard mobile phone than use one that was especially designed for them. We'll work through the tradeoffs and pitfalls of solving other people's dilemmas, and ask what it means to do good in a world where ignorance fuels the fight against exploitation as much as it buttresses the perpetration of injustice.

While the chapters herein will at times stand on each other's shoulders, the path we'll take is more of a crisscross than a straight line. The lessons and techniques I'll describe can be taken piecemeal, and in whatever order you may choose to read them, but they're best absorbed as a complete prism rather than separate and distinct lenses onto the world. By the end, I hope you'll see the chaos and flux of humanity with a sharper focus. In the process you may catch a glimpse of the future, or of possible futures, but most important, you'll gain a new set of tools to prepare your business for the future.

Chapter 1

Crossing State (of Mind) Lines

You and I may never have met before. I have no idea where you are or how you're consuming this book. I will, however, venture a guess: wherever you may be reading this, you're not doing it in the shower. If I'm wrong, well, bravo for you. But if I'm right, my question to you is this: why *aren't* you in the shower right now?

It may seem like a dumb question, but in design research it's exactly the sort of foundational inquiry that allows us to get at the core of user behavior. Unless you're designing wedding rings or pacemakers, there's no such thing as a 24-7-365 user. My colleagues and I spend a great deal of time thinking about touchpoints—the times and places where users would likely be interacting with the product or service we're designing—and triggers that would prompt users to act in one way or another during those times and in those places. These factors can highlight new opportunities to serve unmet needs, or to better tailor products and services to fit the circumstances in which customers use them. But in order to understand touchpoints and triggers, we have to take into account the boundaries that separate use from disuse—the border between doing and don't-ing.

Let's take this mind-set to a café, where most people would look around and see a bunch of people seated at tables drinking coffee, chatting, and typing on laptops. An inquisitive researcher, however, might ask why none of them are in the restroom, why anyone would even want to go to the restroom, or even whether it would behoove management to provide free diapers for customers.

Questions like these, however dumb they may seem, allow us to outline the parameters of user behavior—and human behavior. We ask these questions because we know that behavior isn't simply dictated by the laws of nature and the laws of states, but also by cultural norms, social contexts, interpersonal relationships, personalities, and perceptions. When we look at any behavior, even something as mundane as a trip to the restroom, we can uncover all sorts of factors at play. Our goal is to put the parameters of behavior into perspective. And in order to paint the proper picture, we need to put it in the proper frame.

The Frame Job

Over the course of a corporate field study, it's common to collect a great deal of information from participants about the minutiae of their lives: from what time they get up in the morning to the last thing they do before closing their eyes at night; where and with whom they hang out; where they go shopping; what they wear; why they prefer one brand over another; with whom they communicate and why. Some of it may be quite valuable, some entirely trivial, and we use a variety of techniques to help us figure out what matters. When we move from collecting all this information into analyzing and synthesizing it, we are looking to do two things: make sense of our observations and then reveal patterns and trends that we believe are accurate enough to share with our clients.

To a client or outside observer, design ideas that aren't presented within a research-based, real-world framework can seem arbitrary. For organizations that were weaned on quantitative market research, it's not enough to be inspired—they want to be able to trace that inspiration back to its source.

A multilayered synthesis process runs throughout every field study. During an interview, the questions evolve from those that build a foundational understanding to ones that include more inferred assumptions. As soon as we finish an interview or other data collection session, the team members assemble in the nearest café and review the data we've collected, working to build a shared understanding of what we thought was relevant. Data, like milk, is best consumed fresh; the longer we take to analyze it, the more likely we are to lose the thread that connects it to its original meaning. At some point in the day the team heads back to our "mission control," most often a room in a hotel, guesthouse, or home, where the walls are papered with notes and ideas. Before leaving the city, while we still have access to our local team, we like to spend a full day sifting through the data. Later, back at the studio, we might spend a week or two in a project room surrounded by the data pinned to the wall on giant foam boards, where the team systematically processes it through different lenses.

At this stage, we need to begin organizing the data into a cohesive framework, but the right one—one that creates order out of the chaos of data, setting all the little statements, events, and outcomes to a story—is rarely easy to find.* A good framework helps the researcher accomplish several things: it tells a big truth, substantiated by all the important data and contradicted by none of it; it often maps behaviors across space and/or time; it captures the different behaviors across a range of individuals, taking into account idiosyncrasies without overgeneralizing them; and it creates a narrative around causes and effects, so that reasonable assumptions can be made if anyone tries to throw a "what-if" at it. If someone can glance at it, understand it with minimal explanation, incorporate it into their worldview, and then use it to contemplate new scenarios, then it's working.

If there's such a thing as a default framework in corporate research, it's the customer journey map, which provides detailed information about each event in a customer's typical day, diagrams how she moves from one event to another, and identifies all the touchpoints where she may use the product or service we're designing. Customer journey maps tend to be very precise in their documentation and technical in their appearance— many boxes connected by many lines. They're useful for building a basic level of understanding, and certainly no one would accuse them of being arbitrary, but reading them can sometimes feel like a mechanical process.

---

* http://www.servicedesigntools.org offers a nice collection of frameworks and other tools used in design research, along with some simple case studies.

There are numerous alternatives to the customer journey map, but there is one in particular, less commonly used but phenomenally useful when applied skillfully, that can bring the diffuse spectrum of almost any human behavior into focus: the threshold map.

Threshold mapping allows us to map out "default" conditions—the normal state a person experiences a majority of the time (for example, most people feel clean enough throughout the day that they won't drop whatever they're doing and hop in the shower if it's available)—and then understand what happens when a person crosses the line into an alternative condition. Often, the feelings that people experience as they approach or cross a threshold lead them to think and act differently.

Design studios, workshops, and laboratories are good at testing and exploring what their products are capable of and what they can withstand when users put them through the wringer of everyday life. Most warranties are predicated on "normal wear and tear," and you can bet a team of researchers spent a good deal of time defining "normal." But increasingly companies around the globe are looking to inform design with greater insight into the makings of their users, not just their products, and what drives use in the first place. And in order to understand behavior, we need to get out of the lab and into people's natural environs.

Often, when people cross a threshold from one state into its alternative, or when they avoid crossing that boundary by taking an action to steer themselves away from the borderline, it's a matter of maintaining standards of acceptability and appropriateness. For designers to understand what lies within the boundaries of acceptable use and what lies outside those bound-aries, they need to understand the contexts in which things will be used, and the range of likely conditions that will change that context in some way.

In the same way that a testing laboratory can help us under-stand the boundary between normal and extreme (and probably out-of-warranty) use of a product, design research helps us un-derstand the boundaries of normal behaviors. And one of the strongest ways of communicating normal and outlier behavior is through a threshold diagram.

Threshold Mapping 101

Thresholds can teach us a great deal about the ways people make decisions based on their physical and mental states, and what they do to maintain or regain a particular state. To give you a quick rundown of the basics, I'll walk you through a simple ex-ample by mapping a threshold you manage every day, all the time: hunger.

Imagine, for a moment, a day in your life as a horizontal timeline, with 12:01 a.m. at one end of that line and midnight at the other. Mark off when you get up and when you go to sleep (and assuming for now that you won't wake until morning once you're asleep). So that we have some context, plot the different places that you go during the day, and the time you spend there: home, your commute, work, the café where you like to lunch, the grocery store you shop at on the way home, and then home again. On top of this, plot the moments when you eat, whether a meal or a snack. The vertical axis, in this case, indicates your level of hunger. Now plot three lines along the timeline: your level of hunger, as it varies throughout the day; a peak threshold, above which you may be so well sated that you can't even bear the thought of another morsel of food; and a trough threshold, below which you would be too hungry to function. The area between the two thresholds is your comfort zone, and in normal circumstances you'll do what it takes to stay within that zone.

Unless you like to eat to the verge of stomach rupture or fast until you're just about dead from starvation, these thresholds are not absolutes. Moreover, they are not straight lines. They shift up and down throughout the day as you navigate various contexts, with the trough rising as you recognize the need for brain food before a big exam or sinking as you climb into bed too tired to address the rumble in your midsection.

Your hunger level is of course not static, either, gradually veering toward the trough as you go an increasing length of time without eating. If you're proactive, and conscientious about staying within your comfort zone, you'll see the trough coming and eat something as you near it but before you reach it. You'll also stop eating before you reach the peak. It's a neat, simple pattern that anyone can visualize.

But it's also not a realistic one for most people. There are many moments where the normal rules won't apply: you wake up late for work, pick up breakfast at the café next to your office, and give in to the temptation to buy one of their famous bagels; you're stuffed from lunch but it's a coworker's birthday and you feel social pressure to accept a slice of chocolate cake; or you leave work late and find yourself at the grocery store with a shopping cart full of comfort food, due to a combination of hunger and all the tantalizing smells of fresh, sweet dough emanating from the bakery. Your own comfort zone probably shifted just from reading that last sentence, although the extent of the shift will likely depend on whether you've just eaten.

The thresholds change even more drastically when you consider an extreme event like devout fasting for Ramadan or ritualistic gorging on Thanksgiving. All those external forces can make a mess of what might otherwise be nicely systematic behavior, but the beauty of the threshold map is that it can take those moments into consideration, plot them and their outcomes, and still provide a clear picture—no matter how jagged the three lines get.

We can also map different threshold diagrams for different types of people: how would a hunger threshold diagram differ for a twenty-year-old athlete versus a forty-five-year-old office worker? How would it differ for a successful dieter versus a compulsive eater?

It's a simple exercise but one that can deliver a large payoff, revealing both a richer understanding of *what* people *are and are not* doing, what triggers them to go outside their zone of comfort, and more important, *why*. The format also allows an audience to rapidly absorb the basics, and supports an incredible level of depth and storytelling, particularly around the exceptions.

Exceptions to the Rules

For many people, the comfort zone is an ideal, normalized state, and like anything else that people call "normal," it comes wrapped in a set of social and personal assumptions that can reveal someone's worldview. It also inherently suggests that there is an "abnormal," a state that lies on the other side of some boundary, a state that may be considered extreme, where one might not venture by choice. The abnormal state is most likely an uncomfortable one (in our example feeling bloated or excessively hungry), and someone who falls into it is likely to try to get out of it as quickly as possible. Like a product testing lab exploring what will trigger a product to break, understanding what it takes for someone to move to an extreme can be just as revealing. In my experience, companies have a reasonable understanding of what is normal but struggle with the extremes, which means they don't understand the tensions that pull normal in different directions.

Just think: How uncomfortable do you get when you haven't checked your email for an hour? How many minutes do you have to spend at the gym before you decide it's okay to have a cupcake later on? How long does a shirt have to go unworn before you decide to give it away? How annoying does that half-broken thing in your house need to be before you'll finally get around to fixing it? Understanding the exceptions and the behaviors needed to bring you back into the comfort zone often reveals little things that might turn out to not be so little: a tweaked interface for prioritizing missed communication; a new pricing model for using exercise machines; how recycling used clothing can free up room in the cupboard and trigger new purchasing behaviors; or a distributed model for sharing DIY tools in the neighborhood.

Such thresholds are fundamental factors in decisionmaking, whether we explicitly set them or not. Sticking to them, however, is another matter, and a great deal of research has gone into uncovering how and why people miss their marks, so to speak.

Casinos are especially adept at coaxing patrons out of their comfort zones and into risk-taking by plying them with alcoholic drinks, free meals, and massive doses of oxygen. Psychological experiments on willpower have shown that hunger, lack of sleep, and decision fatigue (the mental toll exacted by extensive decision-making) can all derail otherwise steadfast commitments to self-discipline. Consumer psychologists tell us about how seemingly innocuous distractions, from sound snippets to lighting, promote impulsive, irrational buying habits. In Richard Thaler and Cass Sunstein's book *Nudge: Improving Decisions About Health, Wealth, and Happiness*, the authors argue that people can be coaxed into making better (or at least more classically rational) decisions through "choice architecture," creating defaults and subtle encouragements that suggest one direction of action without compelling it. These are but a few of the countless examples of research on the pliability of ordinary behavior.

What does it all have to do with threshold mapping? Design research is very good at exploring the many different variables that impact changes in behavior, and the aforementioned examples suggest that those parameters are constantly shifting, albeit in ways that can often be anticipated. A threshold map, whether derived from quantitative or qualitative data, allows you to account for these parameter shifts—even when there's no noticeable change in behavior. It can also highlight the times and places where a person is right on the cusp of change and therefore most susceptible to manipulation. So the next time you're in cupcake avoidance mode, be mindful of not only how hungry you are, but also what's going on around you that could bump up your trough threshold and change your mind before you know it. And if you're the one selling the cupcakes, just look for the hungry, tired, and mentally weary passersby and give 'em a nudge.

So Fresh and So Clean

Let's go back to the earlier question: why aren't you in the shower right now? Looking at it through the lens of thresholds, the simple answer is that you're within your comfort zone, somewhere above the (trough) threshold of discomfort. But what would it take to push you below that threshold? And what would it take to push you above your peak threshold, into the zone of maximum confidence? In one study my team and I conducted on behalf of a large, upscale personal care brand, we used these questions to frame our data and show the client how its customers really went about their daily grooming.

In several large Asian cities, we interviewed people at great length about their grooming habits and all the motivations and consequences that play into those habits. We learned about their home lives, their social lives, their love lives, and their work lives, and the pressures they faced in each. We learned when they brushed their hair and when they brushed their teeth. We learned about the difference between taking a bath and standing in front of the sink, the nuanced difference between the dynamics of a morning shower and an evening one. We traveled their morning and evening commuting routes. With all that information, we were able to outline a typical weekday and weekend day for each participant, and then cluster the participants into different archetypes based on their dominant motivations for grooming: getting a date, climbing the corporate ladder, managing stigmas like body odor or bad breath, and so on.

Each archetype had distinctly nuanced habits. The date-seeker might have spent upward of an hour in front of the mirror before hitting the clubs on a Saturday night, whereas the ambitious worker might have popped a breath mint every time the boss walked by. Another archetype, the carefree coaster, might not groom at all until he sensed that his unkemptness was actively repelling people. They all took steps to stay within their own desired comfort zones, but the dimensions of those zones looked very different when we plotted them out.

In threshold mapping, we use the term "comfort zone" loosely to describe the area where a person maintains the status quo for everyday life, going about business as usual, which typically means not engaging in the behavior we're studying. We could just as well call it the "peace of mind" zone or the "generally okay" zone, because ultimately the barometer for behavior is one's own perception.

With the grooming study, we found that the desire for cleanliness had generally little to do with physical comfort and almost everything to do with social acceptability and self-confidence. Many of the participants expressed little interest in any form of grooming while they spent extended periods of time at home alone. The majority of their grooming efforts at home came in anticipation of social encounters; their efforts outside the home generally took place at times when they developed some anxiety about impending embarrassment and felt the need to correct course somehow.

This qualitative data suggested that the trough threshold for grooming exists at the point where someone is unwilling to engage in any social interaction (or some specific interaction at that point, like a meeting or a date) without first freshening up somehow. The zone below that threshold is effectively the "zone of shame." At the other end of things, the peak threshold lies at the point of maximum confidence, where people feel like they're so eminently presentable that they can interact with absolutely anyone, from supermodels to heads of state.

When someone falls below a trough, especially in a situation where resources are limited (for example, no toothbrush, shower, or change of clothes readily available), the objective is not to aim for the peak or even a happy middle ground, but simply to find some way to climb back up above the trough, and to do so quickly. It could be as simple as a breath mint and packaging that declares that it "kills bad breath," a splash of cold water on the face, a quick makeup touch-up, or even a reassuring compliment from a friend—whatever it takes to feel, at the very least, adequate. They might not be as thorough as the elaborate rituals one goes through to reach maximum confidence, but the motivations are very different: looking and feeling just acceptable enough to come out of hiding, versus carefully achieving perfection. A shrewd marketer would recognize this difference and see the equivalent messages: "you don't have to be a hermit, and it doesn't take much" versus "you could be a star."

When we look at the parameters of any user behavior through the lens of thresholds, especially within a specific city, country, or other cultural context, social standards are like an aperture that expands and contracts the comfort zone. If you think about the standards of dress in a typical office in Silicon Valley, there's a very wide band of acceptability—it's okay to wear chinos, it's okay to have visible tattoos, it's even okay to be a bit scruffy. Conversely, in a Japanese corporate environment, the definition of an acceptable appearance is much stricter and therefore creates a much tighter comfort zone. A corporate salaryman is expected to wear a particular shade of suit, particular kinds of shoes and shirts, and maintain his appearance regardless of physical discomfort. The band is so narrow that when the Japanese government instituted energy-saving air-conditioning policies that raised the average office temperature in summer to around 82 degrees Fahrenheit, they had to launch a concurrent marketing campaign prodding workers to lose their suit jackets and neckties (and telling bosses not to fire their subordinates for this otherwise inappropriate conduct).*

If you want to compare behavior across cultures, it can be particularly useful to see what happens when you take one person's habits (his level-of-functioning line) and expand or contract his comfort zone according to different cultural constraints. For instance, what would be considered a socially acceptable level of body odor for a manual laborer in rural Nepal, and what would it be for his cousin, a schoolteacher in the urban hub of Kathmandu? This can give you some sense of what behaviors would change, as well as where and when they would be trig-

---

* Actually it took two attempts to get Japanese workers to buy into the idea: the "Cool Biz" campaign in 2005 and then "Super Cool Biz" in 2011.

gered. Likewise, if you're traveling across cultures, especially for business (or for any other reason that has you set on impressing the locals), you'd be wise to look into the cultural benchmarks for things like dress and grooming, money carrying, and even acceptable levels of drunkenness, and consider how to calibrate your own thresholds accordingly.

Riotous or Righteous

So far, we've focused strictly on threshold maps as frameworks for the motives and actions of individuals. But just as mapping thresholds opens windows into so many underlying aspects of individual behavior, it can also do the same for our understanding of collective behavior, according to sociologist Mark Granovetter.

In the late 1970s, Granovetter sought to unravel a very tricky question: if a crowd of people is assumed to behave according to accepted social norms yet deviates from those standards, is it because the unwritten rules of society have suddenly changed, or because diverse individual motives have conspired to produce unexpected consequences? He outlined two hypothetical scenarios, both involving crowds of 100 people gathered in a public square, teetering on chaos. In one scenario, a single instigator decides to break a window, which inspires a second rock-thrower, then a third, and so on, until a full-scale riot has broken out. Granovetter imagines the newspaper headline: "A crowd of radicals engaged in riotous behavior." In the other scenario, that first rabble-rouser still breaks a window, but the violence ends there. This time the headline reads, "A demented troublemaker broke a window while a group of solid citizens looked on." So what accounts for the near-total change in collective action? Do 99 ne'er-do-wells suddenly become peaceniks? Actually, as Granovetter explains, only one of them does—by the slimmest of moral margins.

You see, each individual in the crowd makes a personal decision to riot or not, based on perceptions about the benefits of rioting (a cathartic release of anger) versus the risks (the possibility of arrest). Aside from the instigator, who is willing to riot no matter what, every other member of the crowd seeks a certain safety in numbers. The more radical ones might follow the lead of the instigator, and perhaps a few others thereafter, while the more conservative ones will wait until nearly everyone else is involved before they too join in. These are their thresholds—the number of others they are willing to follow. For the instigator, the threshold is 0; for the most conservative person out of the 100, the threshold is 99 (no room for totally staunch abstainers in this hypothetical).

In the first scenario presented, the distribution of thresholds is completely even. After the instigator, the person with a threshold of 1 (that 1 being the instigator) throws the second rock, followed by the person with a threshold of 2, then the person with a threshold of 3, and so on, until everyone has joined in. However, in the second scenario, there are two people with a threshold of 2 and none with a threshold of 1. After the instigator gets things started, both of those threshold 2s look around to see where that second rock will come from so they can throw theirs, but that second rock never comes. Even though 99 out of 100 people carry the same inclinations, their thresholds are unmet and a completely different situation unfolds.

Granovetter's model is purely hypothetical, and even as such you could argue that if the one little shift occurs at threshold 98 instead of threshold 1, the two outcomes would end up roughly the same. Still, it illustrates the notion that a given set of individual motives, especially ones that depend heavily on context, can lead to widely varying outcomes—for individuals and for groups.* As investment firms like to remind us in their disclaimers, past performance is no guarantee of future results.

Many of us, however, are in the business of future results. We want to change the world, make the next big thing, put a ding in the universe. On the surface, a threshold map may not seem like much help. You could say it's a reactive instrument, constructed with details from past and present experiences, generally focused on a typical day-in-the-life rather than the course of that life itself. But whatever it may lack in prescience, it makes up for with perspective. By charting the boundaries of normal/acceptable/preferable behavior and the consequences of crossing those lines, we can focus on creating new tools to help people define their thresholds, stay aware of them, stay within them, and even extend them.

---

* In further works, Granovetter would go on to demonstrate how individual thresholds affect such complex group dynamics as racial diversity in residential neighborhoods and the role of popularity in consumer demand.

Threshold-Mapping the Future

There's no such thing as a smooth trajectory when it comes to design evolution, but from a threshold mind-set there does appear to be this pattern: designers first have to establish that a threshold exists, then pinpoint it, figure out how to maintain it, and try to expand the comfort zone. Consider the ways people have managed thresholds of sleep over the course of history.

The great philosopher Plato was renowned for his discourses at dawn, launching into dialectics before the sun reached the sky. The timing posed a challenge for both master and students: sundials might be good timekeepers, but they're rather useless when there's no sun overhead. Instead, Plato used a machine that measured time overnight by the gradual trickling of water, sounding an organ after enough water had passed through it. The device wasn't particularly accurate, but it set a common threshold for socially acceptable behavior among the Academy's students. For all we know, Plato could have coined the phrase "You snooze, you lose"; perhaps Aristotle showed up late that day, missed the lesson, and never passed it along.

Fast-forward a couple of millennia, when the Industrial Revolution redefined the consequences of oversleeping. A factory couldn't begin work until everyone showed up, and thus the threshold of waking up on time became more rigid. Mechanical alarm clocks were introduced to the masses, but early versions proved unreliable, or at least unreliable enough to provide a legitimate excuse for latecomers. The mechanical apparatus didn't do the trick, but factory bosses still needed a tool to enforce punctuality. The simple solution was to employ a "knocker-up," someone who would go around to factory workers' homes and knock on their doors and windows to make sure they were awake.

Since then, we've conquered the obstacle of time accuracy. We know precisely where our thresholds are for maximum sleep, but we've discovered that quality of sleep often diminishes as we near those thresholds. To keep us within our comfort zones, we now have alarm clocks and apps like Sleep Cycle that stir us in the most gentle and pleasant ways possible, analyzing our sleep patterns to calculate the moments when we'll rouse most easily.

Now that we've established a sleep threshold, pinpointed it, and figured out how to stay comfortable inside it, the next step is to manipulate it. In a way, we've been doing so for ages with caffeine, but we heavy coffee drinkers know you still can't out-run sleep. However, military researchers have found that administering a dose of a brain hormone called orexin A allowed monkeys deprived of sleep for up to thirty-six hours to perform as well on cognitive tests as their well-rested peers. In ten years, will we find ourselves hanging out in orexin A cafés for days on end? And what will be the social pressures on people who choose not to take the drug but live in a world of thirty-hour workdays? If it seems far-fetched, just ask a doctor, nurse, long-haul trucker, or fighter pilot how they feel about it.

Let's look into some of the ways threshold models could help us design better services in an ecosystem we all inhabit: the world of money.

In 2009, while I was at Nokia, I conducted a study on mobile money services for emerging markets. At the time, approximately

3.5 billion people around the world lacked access to financial services, but among them roughly half owned mobile phones. Nokia was developing a phone-based system, called Nokia Money, in which users could hand over cash to a merchant and get the digital equivalent deposited on their phones to use for mobile payments, person-to-person transfers, and general safe-keeping.*

For the study, we traveled to China, Indonesia, and Malaysia: interviewing manual laborers on the street, visiting housewives in their homes, and talking to people on every rung of the socio-economic ladder to get a sense of how they spent, saved, and carried money. We asked if they carried wallets, and why or why not. We asked how much cash they were willing to have on them at any time, how they felt when carrying an abnormally large amount, and how they felt when they were running low. We asked how they averted risks, and not just in terms of robbery. How did they avoid overspending, and how did they avoid getting caught out with no cash and no way to get more?

Many of the participants had reserve strategies. If their wallets ran dry, they would have a small amount of cash—a cash cache, if you will—stashed somewhere else (sometimes in a sock, sometimes in a separate pocket, and sometimes, in places with high theft risk, sewn directly into an article of clothing) that could tide them over until they made it home, to a bank, or to an ATM. What was particularly interesting about the cash cache was that people used it to both frighten themselves and assuage their panic. An empty wallet is a scary thing to look into: a sign

---

* Nokia Money was first rolled out across India in 2011.

that a very weighty threshold has been reached. But instead of that threshold being one of "I have no money—how the hell do I get home/get food/get by now?" it's only a threshold of alarm. If I have a cash cache, I know that my empty wallet doesn't spell doom—it simply means it's time to act, and spend, differently.

An empty wallet is a strong and very concrete feedback mechanism for cash transactions. On the less tangible side, psychologists have found that people with any hint of miserly tendencies use a feedback system in the area of the brain known as the insula, which generates feelings of disgust when we encounter an unpleasant odor, a horrid picture, or, it seems, a budget-shattering pair of Bruno Magli shoes.

But when we use credit cards, debit cards, and mobile wallets, we don't get to peer into the void of a wallet, and we can't always count on our insulae to steer us right. This is where good service design comes in.

The website Mint.com is entirely geared toward helping users navigate the threshold of alarm. It allows anyone to consolidate all their bank accounts, credit cards, investments, and bills into one place, then set budgets and financial goals. When budgets are exceeded, account balances run low, large transactions are made, or suspicious activity takes place, Mint.com can send an alert. The service has become so popular that it created market pressure on banks, which turn healthy profits when customers overshoot their limits, to offer similar alerts.

We know this threshold exists, and now we have ways of actively demarcating it. What sorts of tools can we design in the future to help people stay within their comfort zones? What sorts of tools could even expand those comfort zones? Perhaps someone will devise a system that can learn your product preferences and your budget, then create shopping lists that satisfy both—or better yet, automatically ship things to you.

The potential for innovation also lies at the other end of the spending comfort zone: the threshold of concern. Every time you face a spending decision, you're expending some amount of cognitive energy, paying what's known in behavioral economics as a mental transaction cost. When that psychological toll surpasses the value of the purchase itself, you've reached the threshold of concern. This is why many web-based micropayment systems have failed—even if you're willing to spend a penny every time you feel like looking at Photoshopped images of cats in outer space, you probably don't want to have to think about that penny every time you spend it. It's also why people prefer subscriptions to piecemeal payments and why they pay restaurant checks with credit cards even when they have enough cash to cover (the ethereal depletion of funds carries a lower mental transaction cost than the physical depletion).

Attacking the threshold of concern is merely a matter of finding ways to wipe out that mental transaction cost. One way to do so is by delegating it. Imagine your car being linked into your city's parking system—it knows where every available parking space is, and how much each space costs. Rather than asking you if you'd prefer to walk two extra blocks to save a dollar, it makes the decision for you based on your general preference for either saving money or parking as close as possible to your destination. When you park, there's no meter to feed; your car either charges it to your credit card or debits the money from a smart account that you've loaded up with cash.

Can I say with any certainty that the future will look like this? Absolutely not. Thresholds and threshold maps are only tools to help us frame what we observe in the present—and an understanding of the present is a hell of a good starting point for thinking about and designing the next.

Chapter 2

The Social Lives
of Everyday Objects

In the early days of ancient Rome, the toga was the national gar-
ment, worn by men, women, and children alike, across social
classes. Its universality made it difficult to make any statements
like "I'm hip, young, and fashionable" or "I'm a deal-making,
power-brokering machine," although magistrates and high priests
liked to embellish theirs with a purple stripe around the border
to make their eminence evident. But by the second century BC,
the toga had become strictly a status symbol for men conducting official business. Sumptuary laws were established, explicitly stating who could or could not wear certain togas or use
certain dyes. Women were banned from wearing togas entirely,
except for prostitutes, who were forced to wear them as manifest stigma. And no one—aside from kings and, later, emperors—
was allowed to wear a completely purple toga, the ultimate
symbol of power.

It may seem arbitrary to take a simple everyday item and
suddenly imbue it with powerful symbolism, but in our modern

culture of branding and conspicuous consumption, just about every product on our shelves can be construed as some metaphor for personal identity. We use the word *superficial* pejoratively to describe people who are overly concerned with such symbols, yet we're all concerned with them to some degree, because we all use objects—from overt ones like jewelry and cars to subtle ones like the reading material we stock in our bathrooms—as tools to communicate aspects of our selves. And while we may not be subject to fines and imprisonment for wearing the wrong clothes, like the Romans were, we live by unwritten social rules that govern how we dress, how we decorate our homes, and even how we check the time.

We know the rules when we're in our usual contexts, but once we step into an unfamiliar social situation the rules can completely flip on us. The same Gucci suit that helps you land a cushy job in a corporate firm could attract derision as hoity-toity when worn in a dive bar. Is it any surprise that the word *taboo*, in its Tongan roots, is used to mean both "forbidden" and "sacred"?

The code of cool versus uncool, classy versus gauche, trash versus treasure is at times flimsy, at other times indecipherable. Clueless consumer brands expect trendspotters to figure out what the hippest kids are doing, thinking, and wearing, and whether it will spread to the masses. Some people think this is what I do, but there's a difference between what I do and what trendspotters do. Trends can be valuable indicators of the zeitgeist, but the people who set them and follow them will invariably bounce from one trend to the next because, on a fundamental level, they're driven by a desire to stay current.

While trendspotters look at the more immediate patterns, my clients are more interested in understanding underlying and usually more permanent desires and other factors that affect how people present themselves. When people put their personal objects on display, it's as if they're inviting you through a doorway into their selves—who they are, who they think they are, and who they want you to think they are. But before you walk into that edifice, you have to get a sense of the neighborhood in which it sits.

Looking the Part

In *The Presentation of Self in Everyday Life*, sociologist Erving Goffman's seminal analysis of social dynamics, Goffman describes interactions in terms of dramatic performance, in which every individual involved plays dual roles of performer and audience. Like a stage drama, every performance is carried out within a setting and revolves around a scene—the situation. Any performer can attempt to define a situation, but things can get awkward if there's not a consensus. Imagine sitting in the car with a friend and a popular song comes on the radio: do you rock out to it, or change the channel? Maybe you don't like the song but your friend absolutely loves it and defines the situation right away, so for the sake of camaraderie you swallow your pride and break out your air guitar. Some situations have preestablished definitions and codes of behavior, and it is assumed that everyone involved knows how to perform appropriately. In this sense, rudeness is simply a matter of staging the wrong performance in the wrong scene. Goffman cites a report on seamen in the 1940s returning home and forgetting to shed their maritime manners, such as one who told of accidentally asking his mother to "pass the fucking butter."

In 2005, while at Nokia, I decided to test out this idea: that an object dripping with status symbolism, when brought into an undefined situation without being brandished in a performance of posh extravagance, would fail to define the situation or my status by itself. I was in New York on business, looking for a temporary workspace, and a colleague set me up with a desk at the offices of Vertu, the high-end mobile phone brand and independent subsidiary of Nokia. When Vertu launched in 2002, *Wired* reported that "the first devices, costing a staggering 24,000 euros ($21,240), will be cased in platinum, display a sapphire crystal glass screen and offer a sound as clear as a Mozart symphony, Vertu said in connection with the company's launch in Paris during the fashion show week." As Hutch Hutchison, Vertu's head of design, told the *Financial Times* about the brand's origin, "The idea was that the individual who would put this telephone on the table during a meeting would be regarded as the most powerful person in the room." This I had to see.

As I was leaving the Vertu office, I jokingly asked if I could borrow one of their phones for a test run. Shockingly (not least because I go through tech gear like other people go through underwear), they agreed and fetched one from a locked drawer. What I didn't tell them was that I'd be taking it to Japan, where they had yet to launch, and where their GSM-configured phone would be rendered incommunicado by the country's 3G network infrastructure. All I could do with the thing, aside from using it as a doorstop, was to manually trigger the ringtones—or try to figure out whether it could live up to Hutchison's billing in a place where only very early adopters of international status objects would have any awareness or appreciation of it.

I took the Vertu phone to several cafés in the upscale Daikanyama neighborhood of Tokyo and placed it strategically on my table to see what kind of reaction it would draw. There's a tribe of early-adopting Japanese with noses for high fashion, design, and art that would make a truffle hound whimper, and yet even in these places where social norms allowed people to safely leave luxury items out to show off, and for strangers to approach one another to chitchat about whatever caught their eye, none of them sniffed out its workmanship or sticker value even if it was "worth" about nine months' wages for the average Japanese worker. Who knows whether they were regarding me as the most powerful person in the room, but they certainly weren't lining up to kiss my ring(tone).

One of the things about the Vertu that both fascinated and disgusted me in equal measure was that beneath the titanium, sapphire, and glass exterior, here was a $20,000 phone with an almost identical circuit board and user interface to what you'd find on a device that cost a hundredth of the price. Part of Vertu's value proposition is its exclusivity, one-to-one boutique service, and the idea that their phones are crafted by phone ateliers for the most discerning clientele. But is it all worth the price tag? That is to say, in the classical economic world of supply and demand, would any rational consumer fork over $20,000 for a phone when the next-cheapest option on the market costs about $19,000 less?

The answer is of course not—but then, we don't live in a classical economic fantasyland. We live in a world of Veblen goods, such as Vertu phones, for which demand paradoxically increases as their prices increase. The "Veblen effect" was coined in 1950 by economist Harvey Leibenstein, who pointed out that consumer demand depended not only on the functional utility of goods but also on certain social factors: a desire to be "in style" (the "bandwagon effect"); a desire to stand out from the herd (the "snob effect"); and a desire for "conspicuous consumption," a term introduced a half-century earlier by sociologist Thorstein Veblen.

In *The Theory of the Leisure Class*, Veblen outlined the social equation used by ruling classes to differentiate themselves from their subjects, and by wealthy individuals to assert their superiority to one another. "In order to gain and to hold the esteem of men it is not sufficient merely to possess wealth or power," Veblen wrote. "The wealth or power must be put in evidence, for esteem is awarded only on evidence. And not only does the evidence of wealth serve to impress one's importance on others and to keep their sense of his importance alive and alert, but it is of scarcely less use in building up and preserving one's self-complacency." *Consumam, ergo sum.*

The accoutrements of status are about establishing an identity, but they are also about relative identity, and extravagance is one way for the rich to show they have the means to do what the poor cannot. As Veblen so acerbically remarked, "Throughout the entire evolution of conspicuous expenditure, whether of goods or of services or human life, runs the obvious implication that in order to effectually mend the consumer's good fame it must be an expenditure of superfluities. In order to be reputable it must be wasteful. No merit would accrue from the consumption of the bare necessities of life, except by comparison with the abjectly poor who fall short even of the subsistence minimum; and no standard of expenditure could result from such a comparison, except the most prosaic and unattractive level of decency."

Cynical as he may have been, Veblen was very much on point about two things: the pursuit of status requires evidence to support one's cause; and ostentation, vulgar as it may seem, is rather strong evidence that someone isn't poor. However, as researchers in the Netherlands have found, extravagance can actually confer much more than an aura of wealth.

In a series of experiments on the social effects of designer clothing, Rob Nelissen and Marijn Meijers of Tilburg University found that conspicuous designer labels could elicit significantly more job recommendations, greater amounts of money collected for charity, and higher levels of cooperation in money-sharing games. When they sent a research assistant to a shopping mall to solicit participants for a mock survey, 52 percent of people she stopped agreed to take the survey when she was wearing a Tommy Hilfiger–logoed sweater, but only 13 percent did so when she wore an unbranded sweater. The labels, however, didn't always yield positive results. When Nelissen and Meijers told participants in the money-sharing game that they had given the designer shirt to its wearer, thus implying that she didn't necessarily possess the wealth and taste to purchase it for herself, the shirt no longer had any effect. It was no longer a genuine representation of status. But as I've found in my work, authenticity isn't necessarily what counts—just the appearance of it.

In 2007, I was in Bangkok for a study about what women wanted out of mobile phones, and more broadly about what it meant to be a young woman in Thailand. As the other researchers and I interviewed our participants, we strolled with them through Bangkok's endless sea of humidity and whizzing motorbikes. After the workshop we asked a few of the local attendees to take us on a tour of what they considered to be their perfect day in the city, with enough experiences to be worthy of a separate book. At one point we found ourselves in a relatively poor district, wandering through a pop-up street market filled with hawkers selling everything from produce to sunglasses. We came across one particular stall that stood out, and not because it was selling anything particularly eye-catching. In fact, all it had was a blanket and a makeshift display rack. On the rack were cheap cardboard cards bearing cartoonish images of toothy grins, and running across those teeth were simple wires, tucked in at each end: false orthodontic braces, selling for a mere 39 baht (or about $1.30).

This wasn't a case of a socks merchant making a little extra money on the side from a novelty item. The gentleman selling the ersatz braces had no other offerings, which indicated that demand was more than modest. His stall seemed to get a decent amount of foot traffic, exclusively from adolescent girls. I can't say whether they viewed the braces as a gag or took them seriously, but if they were willing to endure the pain and awkwardness of putting bits of metal in their mouths and wrapping the ends around their teeth, they probably treated that cost as a legitimate investment in their appearance. Of course, fake braces won't straighten anyone's teeth, but they can give the impression that those teeth might someday become straightened. More important, they insinuate that the wearer (or more likely her family) has the financial means to afford such luxuries as orthodontics.

The Bangkok braces are a curious case, and not just because braces seem like an unlikely status symbol in the first place, much less the sort of thing one would want to counterfeit. Why would a girl choose to wear false braces as opposed to, say, a knockoff Gucci T-shirt? Perhaps she'd wear both, but in a place like Bangkok, where knockoff designer clothing can be found anywhere and worn by anyone, false braces make a less obvious— and therefore more convincing—ruse.

If braces can be considered a status symbol, does that mean that anything can be one? There are plenty of other examples of unlikely status symbols. In a criminological study of low-socioeconomic-status Hispanic adolescents in the United States, researchers found that weapon carrying could increase one's popularity and social standing. In Iran, where the Islamist regime has instituted a ban on dog ownership, dogs are considered positive symbols of rebellious fortitude among secularists who oppose the government. In the United Arab Emirates, car license plates, especially single-digit ones, have become hot items: in February 2008, the number "1" plate sold at auction for $14.3 million. And all over the world, from Cairo to Chongqing, I've visited third-party mobile phone vendors who charge premiums for phone numbers with auspicious digits or sequences.

You could say it's the market force of superstition, but at heart it's the force of impression management. The phone number is a primary form of identification in many parts of the world, and lucky numbers convey a very different impression than unlucky ones. When the Afghan government began issuing license plates starting with the digits "39," a furor erupted among those who received those plates, because 39 is considered the "pimp number" and therefore highly unsavory. Just as Afghans don't want to be viewed as pimps, especially through a display as public as a license plate, people in most cultures don't want to be viewed as a different kind of pimp: the kind who brashly shows off every symbol of wealth and status in his or her possession. But why do we place this stigma on some people and not others—and why do we place it on some objects and not others?

The Status Game

While conducting a study on mobile money services in Xi'an, China, in 2009, I started to wonder: why do we display or conceal cash, or bank statements, differently from objects that hold the same monetary value? When we go into restaurants, why is it socially acceptable to place your phone (as status symbol) on the table, but it's not okay to take out all your cash and credit cards and spread them out in front of you? Why does it feel so instinctively wrong that we don't even try it? It could be because we think of cash as literally, physically, bacterially dirty, and having that on a food table seems unhygienic. But even credit cards, which seem cleaner and sometimes even reflect some aspects of the owner's personality that she might want to put on display, are generally not allowed on the table.

In keeping with my general belief that it's good to understand why we don't break unwritten rules, instead of just assuming that we can't, I decided to try a little experiment. At dinner with the research team and our local assistants, I asked everyone to lay out all their cash and credit cards on the table. As you can imagine, it was an awkward and uncomfortable experience for all involved, whether they felt like they stood out for having too much or too little cash, too many or too few credit cards, or they were simply nervous about the risk of theft.

Unlike a phone on the table, where there may be a relatively balanced tradeoff between the advantage of easy access (being able to see the screen if a call or message comes in) versus the risk of theft, there is no similar advantage to having money out. Moreover, the notion of easy access creates a valid social excuse for the phone on the table, just as the notion of beauty or style creates a social excuse for expensive clothes and jewelry, and the notion of thrill-seeking creates an excuse for sports cars and wristwatches with built-in altimeters. But there's no legitimate justification for flaunting a wad of cash, unless you're a Rio de Janeiro drug dealer and everyone knows they'll get whacked if they try to steal from you.

For the rest of us, though, a social excuse is important because it allows us to play the game where we pretend to one another that we're not vain. We pretend that we don't care much about social status, because we want to seem approachable. If you walk into a coffee shop in Silicon Valley and stand in line behind someone in jeans and a T-shirt who just stepped out of a beat-up Volvo, for all you know he may be a billionaire who wants to project a "down-to-earth" status.

In Kate Fox's book *Watching the English*, she notes a curious arc in class preferences for "bogside reading," the books and magazines that the English strategically place in their bathrooms for, ahem, extended visits. Working-class folk tend to stock their bogs with light humor (joke books) and sports magazines. Lower-middle-class and middle-middle-class English don't like to have bogside collections, thinking it might come across as vulgar. In contrast, the upper middle class "often have mini-libraries in their loos," carefully curated, sometimes pretentious, but more likely eclectic and "so amusing that guests often get engrossed in them and have to be shouted at to come to the dinner table." Finally, upper-class tastes are remarkably similar to the working class—humor and sports. Only the upper middle class seem at all concerned with impressing their guests, but you could argue that the upper class are showing off all the same, only their aim is to create an air of homeliness amid their stately manors.

English culture is by no means alone in its use of the home as a showroom for status objects, but a middle-class English household, or one in the United States, Europe, or most other parts of the West, is set up much differently from most middle-class Asian homes. Westerners are far more likely to bring guests into their homes than Asians are, for several reasons. In Asian cities, accommodations tend to be far smaller, so there's less space for company to gather, and fewer rooms designed as showpieces for guests (that is, formal dining rooms, guest bathrooms, and guest bedrooms). There's also a stronger culture of dining out; whereas in England or the States there's a wide cost differential between a restaurant meal and a home-cooked one, the margin in China is minimal, so there's less financial motivation to stay in. And traditionally in Asian cities, home ownership rates have been low, so the notion of remodeling and home improvement is a relatively new one, albeit a booming one: in

Shanghai, the rate of home ownership went from 36 percent in 1997 to 82 percent in 2005. But just because people in Asian cultures tend to invest less in showpieces for the home doesn't mean they invest less in showpieces—they're just more likely to buy ones that they can use out in public.

These cultural distinctions naturally lead to different experiences during our research, especially when we conduct home visits. In a Western home, we typically enter through an entrance hall where we might find family photos or other such personal touches; an Asian entryway might be more stripped down to essentials—areas for shoes to be taken off, hooks for keys, and so forth. Westerners are likely to offer "the tour," walking guests from room to room and showing off artworks or other indications of status and taste, whereas in Asian cultures the visit is more likely confined to the living room. In countries like Egypt and Afghanistan, the distinction between guest-friendly and private spaces is even more acute, largely driven by gender divisions. In most cultures the bedroom is off-limits, except perhaps for a quick glance. If you ask to use the bathroom in a Western home you'll likely be directed to a secondary, more ornamental one, not the one primarily used by the residents for washing up. Asian homes, on the other hand, are far more likely to have only one bathroom for the whole house, so you get to see more of what the residents actually use.

In any home visit, East or West, I'm curious to see all the lovely baubles and heirlooms that people are eager to display, but I've found that there's just as much to learn about the residents' tastes and aspirations inside their cupboards and refrigerators. Even if I'm conducting a study on a subject like work-family balance or managing risk, I'll always look for an excuse to see what's in the refrigerator: the brands they buy, the lifestyle choices they make, and how this might underline or contradict the other things they're saying. Fridges and kitchens are the low-hanging fruit of in-home research: they're generally considered neutral for guests to wander into, and the hosts usually assume that there's not too much that can be revealed. Typically the fridge also contains nonfood products such as cosmetics for him and her, or medication. In the freezer, along with what you probably expect, you can find anything from dead rats "for feeding the snake" to stashes of drugs and other illicit goods—never assume people can remember what they own. You can see if the residents are heavy drinkers; if they prefer branded or generic. You can see whether they mind spending an extra dollar on ketchup. You can learn a lot about the value of status from a bottle of Grey Goose in the freezer. Once you reach a certain level of trust with residents, you can ask if the quality is worth the extra money. The answer is usually "I can't tell the difference"; if it's later on in the interview you'll more likely get an "eh, probably not."

The home is certainly a rich environment to get a sense of what people own and why, but sometimes you can learn just as much from the things people *don't* own. One of my favorite contextual research tricks is to go to local photo studios, the kind that people visit to get their portraits taken, sometimes while holding props or standing against fantastical backdrops (or getting them Photoshopped in afterward). Some studios, especially those offering "print club" photo stickers, are adorned with photos of customers—photos that can tell you a great deal about what people would own if they could own whatever they wanted, and where they would go if they could go wherever they wanted. Aside from the occasional Wild West or Victorian getup, the props and backdrops provide valuable clues about real aspirations, whether or not the actual items are realistically attainable for the people holding them. In New Orleans, the object of choice seemed to be a Cadillac; in Mazar-e-Sharif, Afghanistan, it was a reposing lion and a military getup, or the subject suspended on a rope by a military helicopter; all over the world, Ferraris and guns seem to be quite popular.

Perhaps you're wondering why anyone should bother researching people's tastes in things they'll most likely never own. These material fantasies may not be the best indicators of future sales of real Ferraris and lions, but like the braces in Bangkok, they can show you what brands and qualities people want to be associated with, even if they can't have the real thing. Smart merchandisers find ways of generating "masstige," prestige for the masses, by giving aspirants some facet of what they want in a way that fits within spending constraints, creating new markets by developing products that lower the barriers to entry. Just think about how many Ferrari key fobs are out in the world, relative to the number of actual Ferraris.

One of my favorite examples of masstige is the Apple earbuds found in-ear or dangling from the necks of commuters in cities all over the world. They cost about half as much as the cheapest iPod, and perhaps one-tenth as much as an iPhone, but for someone who can't afford the core technology products the earbuds are a gateway into the Apple ecosystem. As former Apple marketing executive Steve Chazin put it, "Wear white headphones and you are a member of the club." Who cares if they're plugged into a cheap knockoff phone in your pocket? It's what's outside that counts.

A Disappearing Act

Now that we're reaching a point where technology is increasingly becoming smaller, invisible, and more connected to things that are out of sight, how will this affect the use of technology to show off social status? In large part, it depends on what values are considered emblematic of status.

Monetary wealth will always have value, but more and more we're valuing time as a precious commodity, and the ability to delegate tasks and conserve time is gaining significance as a sign of status. Additionally, free time, and the freedom to use time autonomously, has increasingly positive connotations. This seems to suggest that as society becomes more hyperconnected, the ability to disconnect and stay disconnected will become a more significant sign of status. If it's increasingly difficult to switch off—to not pick up the phone, to take a three-week vacation—then switching off will become a privilege for the few who can afford to do so.

As I like to say, technology amplifies behavior. It helps those who are trying to do good do more good, and it helps those who are trying to do bad do more bad. If you live in rural Uganda and you or, if you are a male, your wife goes into labor, it's much easier to get a midwife to come help with the birth when you can call her from your mobile phone rather than run six miles to the nearest hospital. And if you're trying to blow up cars, the mobile phone makes a pretty good remote control for an IED (celljammers aside). Following this assumption, technological advances will make it easier for showoffs to show off, easier for high-status individuals to assert their primacy, and harder for those of lower status to escape its fetters.

Imagine a communication device implanted behind the ear that offers 24-7 connectivity. Would it be a symbol of high status or low status? Actually, it could be both, depending on who's using it—and how they use it.

Such a device would allow someone in power to have subordinates closer at hand; at the same time it would subject the subordinates to a greater degree of servitude since they couldn't switch it off. The technology would amplify both roles, but since everyone answers to someone, even if it's their mother, the real status symbol might be the absence of the implant.

Another consequence of miniaturization is that as devices move away from visual interfaces and become strictly audio, the only element of the interface that can be flaunted for status purposes will be the conversation itself. In a way, this is the ultimate in status: if you're speaking into something, where that something is not visible, it can't contradict what you say. It won't call you a liar if you want to say into your audio interface, "Yeah, book me a business-class ticket to Turkey tomorrow. Set up the hotel, and then call Geoffrey and say I won't be able to make the golf club this weekend. Thanks, bye." You could be interacting with your concierge service or talking to your (very confused) calculator app. It's like the old joke about the lawyer who has just moved into a new office. Wanting to impress the first potential client who walks through the door, the lawyer picks up the phone and says, "I'm sorry but I'm just too busy to take your case, not even for thousands of dollars." He hangs up, turns to the man standing before him, and says, "Now, what can I do for you?" "Oh, nothing really," the man replies. "I'm here to connect your telephone."

Designing the Next Status Object

Anyone designing fashion and accessories knows how important it is to decode their market's demand for status symbols that highlight key values like wealth, individuality, and modernity, but the status lens can be just as valuable to someone designing something as mundane as an air conditioner.

In the market for air conditioners, there will be consumers who are driven strictly by utility: "I just want it to work." There are those driven by a combination of utility and frugality: "I want it to work, and I want to pay the absolute minimum for it." They may inform their decisions by brand awareness: "I'm driven by frugality, but I'm not gonna spend a bunch of money on some unknown piece of shit I think is gonna break. I'm gonna spend it on something that I think will be around for a few years." And then there are consumers, and much larger societal segments, who look for brands that share their values, from eco-consciousness to the high life, and allow them to explicitly project those values.

Let's look at China, for example. As I mentioned, home ownership has become a big deal, and with it comes a subsequent investment in the home. Consequently, there's an increase in the value of showing off your home. Before the boom, maybe you lived in a small, crumbling home that you grew up in, and maybe the neighbors who have known you since you were born would pop by, but you wouldn't necessarily invite your college mates by. But today, the home itself, and the notion of it belonging to its residents, has become a symbol of upward mobility. So if the megatrend is that people are increasingly inviting others into their home, it actually matters if they buy an air conditioner that looks utterly utilitarian and functions but is ugly as hell, or the one from the right brand with the right styling. At the same time, for a family buying its first air conditioner, and whose friends and neighbors have never owned one, either, the ugly utilitarian one could still seem mighty impressive.

One of the most effective ways of understanding what people want is to observe, document, and at some point ask them, with the understanding that their answer is framed by their desire to present themselves in a better light, and can itself be an expression of aspirational status. Sometimes the lies can reveal their truth. If you're conducting user research, you definitely want to find out what positive qualities people want to conspicuously project, and what negative ones they want to avoid or hide. Here's a handy umbrella of categories, courtesy of evolutionary psychologist Geoffrey Miller: physical attributes, including health, fertility, and beauty; personality traits, such as conscientiousness, agreeableness, and openness to novelty; and cognitive ones, namely general intelligence.

Equally important is the strength of the desire to project those qualities. Some people are flashier than others, some like to be understated, and some try to avoid status displays altogether. Think about the cumulative sum of all traits, positive and negative, a person displays through objects and appearances— what Goffman would call "performance equipment"—at any given time. Here we can bring back our handy threshold tool and ask: what's the absolute minimum amount of performance equipment you would need in order to leave the house, or in order to have company over? What's the maximum amount of performance equipment you're willing to put on, your peak of extravagance, above which point you would feel too ostentatious and have to tone it down?

Then there are the cultural factors that affect status value, and to understand these we'll need to incorporate a few more lenses, which we'll come to later on. Much like the paradox of the toga in ancient Rome, some objects can connote high status in one culture and low status in another. A suntan on someone who lives in London or New York is a sign to others that that person can afford leisure time, perhaps a tropical vacation, or at least a trip to the tanning salon. On the other hand, a tan in China or Thailand is a mark of peasants who toil in the fields, and the bourgeois are inclined toward whiter skin. Thus on the shelves of pharmacies in Bangkok you'll find dozens of skin products with whitening ingredients; in the United States, expensive moisturizers are tinted. Does this mean that the people who use these products are all that different from one another?

Erving Goffman surely would have agreed with Shakespeare that men and women are merely players who each play many parts in life—only the world is not *a* stage but rather millions of stages, with billions or perhaps trillions of props and costumes. The parts we play, the dialogues we speak, and the gestures we make are only as convincing as their juxtaposition with the scenery on the stages we tread. But the right props and costumes can make us look, and even feel, at home on any given stage.

Chapter 3

Riding the Waves of the Past, Present, and Future

Tokyo's Shinjuku Station during Friday morning rush hour is one of the wonders of the modern world, with heaving swells of suited commuters gliding through lines of ticket barriers, joining a current of suits that takes them out to buses and walkways and on to their offices in government and corporate Japan. Of the 35 million residents of the greater Tokyo metropolitan area, 3.64 million pass through this station, the busiest in the world, every day. It is a sight to behold.

From a vantage point at the edge of the throng (and ideally nursing a decent freshly brewed cup of coffee) you can bear witness to the finessed urban choreography. As they pass through ticket gates, few commuters break stride, reaching forward and placing their bag, wallet, or phone on a pad, letting the object linger just long enough to receive a beep of confirmation as the gates open. Look carefully and you'll see that only a few people this morning are still inserting physical paper tickets, those edifices to a mechanical era. With the vast majority of traffic being daily commuters, most have invested in the digital alternative, the prepaid commuter card, or its mobile equivalent built into the phone.*

The uninterrupted pace is testament to the human ingenuity behind such a system, the ability and desire among commuters to learn and refine an oft-repeated task, and the adaptability of humans willing to try new ways of doing things. Fifteen years ago, all traffic through these gates was either processed mechanically or by a member of the station staff. When you consider the lines at the paper ticket machine and the risk of loss or damage to that small, tearable, crumple-able stub, it should be no surprise that people have invested the time and energy in the digital equivalent.

For the latter part of the twentieth century and the beginning of the twenty-first, Japan has offered a window into global leading-edge behaviors. That unique combination of infrastructure investment and technological ecosystem provides a feast that proves difficult to replicate elsewhere. Japan boasts a tightly integrated high-tech manufacturing base and, perhaps more important, established relationships between people and companies that allow even further integration. The underlying technologies that enable those commuters to pass through ticket gates without breaking step can also be used to buy from vending machines and

----

* Super Urban Intelligent Card (it also sounds like *suika*—or watermelon in Japanese), Suica or Mobile Suica. A few very early adopters also ran experiments with the Suica cards, shaving down their cards' edges and taping them to the inside covers of mobile phones, creating a "mobile ticketing application" before it was truly integrated into the phone.

convenience stores, pick up advertising information,* open key-less lockers in many of Tokyo's stations, pay for taxi rides, and, for a while, shop online via integrated laptops. In a paradoxical clash of old and new, it can also be used to pay for a physical copy of the morning news out of a newspaper box.

In most countries, electronic payment and ticketing systems are primarily sold to consumers on the promise of convenience to oneself, to shave time off the transaction process and to juggle fewer things. In Japan, the benefits of adoption are promoted through another message: that you are less likely to inconvenience others. Consideration for the group over the individual is far more part of the Japanese psyche than in societies such as the United States or Germany, where people generally care less about those around them. (One of the strongest visual reminders of Japanese courtesy comes in winter: in other countries people wear masks to protect themselves from the germs of others; in Japan a sick person wears a mask to protect others from his own germs.)† In this equation, using paper tickets at the ticket gate (or coins at the convenience store checkout) comes with a perceptual risk of being slightly slower and holding everyone else up. As with any other adoption decision that people make for themselves, they do so for personal gain—but as individuals

---

* Suica posters, or SuiPo, are posters that use Suica technology to allow passersby to interact with posters via their Suica cards, in much the same way that people now use QR codes.

† One could argue that not turning up to work in the first place is the greater appreciation for others, but it is certainly less visible reconfirmation of the group. It might apply for heavy colds but less so for something mild.

whose reputations depend on their compliance with social norms, they also do it for the greater good. At the heart of every social pressure is a prod that pushes individuals to do better, do more, or act differently, and perhaps try something new.

For companies looking to bring new products and services to market, understanding the push and pull of adoption—where personal motivations, context, and cultural norms collide—is critical to success. What drives some to adopt early, some late, and some to reject a technology altogether? And how can we use our understanding of this adoption curve to develop, target, and message services in ways that give them the greatest chance of success?

A Breakthrough in the Fields

When we think of the cutting edge, the latest and greatest innovations on the market, our thoughts don't typically turn to corn, that eternal staple of the American heartland. And yet it was from the cornfields of Iowa that our modern concept of how people adopt new offerings and ideas emerged.

In a series of investigations in the 1940s, sociologists Bryce Ryan and Neal Gross of Iowa State University went into two farming communities to study the adoption of hybrid seed corn (cross-pollinated strains of corn intended to produce higher crop yields)—how, when, why, and by whom. From that research, economist Joe Bohlen and sociologist George Beal, both also of Iowa State, crafted a model that has, since its publication in 1957, itself been adopted by countless researchers, analysts, strategists, and academics, well beyond the realm of agriculture.

This model, which Beal and Bohlen called the "diffusion

process," breaks down into five discrete stages that an individual goes through on the path to adoption. First is the awareness stage: the individual learns that the new thing exists, but he may not necessarily know what it is, what it does, and how it works. The awareness stage is then followed by the interest stage: the individual may still not know much about the thing, but he has heard enough to get a sense that it might be useful, and is worth checking out. After interest comes evaluation, a sort of mental test run where the individual imagines the new thing in his life. This is followed by the trial stage, an actual test run.

Finally comes adoption, which Beal and Bohlen defined as "large-scale, continued use of the idea" but more important as "satisfaction with the idea." The distinction is a noteworthy one, because it's easy to get caught in the trap of directly equating adoption with use. It's a fallacy on two fronts: for one, someone may buy a fancy new camera and after a couple of weeks decide to leave it at home and use the camera on her phone instead, yet this doesn't necessarily mean she has given up on the fancy camera (she may simply limit its use to her home and special occasions); and second, for cost-sensitive consumers, there often comes a point where they are no longer satisfied with the idea of the thing they own, like an old flip phone, and have already become satisfied with the idea of something, say an iPhone, that they don't own *yet* but are saving up to buy. If they've already evaluated the iPhone, tested it out, and decided they want it, wouldn't you say they've already adopted the iPhone? At the very least I'd say they've quasi-adopted it.

However, what was most striking about Beal and Bohlen's model, and what has certainly had the most lasting impact, was their breakdown of the "adoption curve": who adopts first, last, and in between. At the forefront are the innovators, who are typically well respected in their communities and have connections outside of their communities that give them exposure to new ideas. Fundamentally, innovators possess a large amount of risk capital—they can afford to try out new things without worrying too much about losing money or prestige if they fail. Innovators are followed by early adopters, who are often younger, well educated, active in the community, and avid media consumers. One of the key drivers for innovators and early adopters is their inherent inquisitiveness, the desire to constantly try new things and experiences. That inquisitiveness can make them wide-ranging dilettantes, or it can lead them to invest large amounts of time in a particular domain and become experts in it. Either way it positions them strategically within subcommunities (networks of video gamers, photographers, etc.), on one hand as people who can introduce new ideas that emerge from other communities, or on the other as the leaders who are the first to know about any new developments in their area of expertise.

If the innovators and early adopters have found clear benefits beyond newness and shininess, the early majority will start to pick up on it. They're often a bit older, perhaps a bit less educated and informed, but typically people with respected opinions. That last point is a tricky one: the early majority can be highly influential, but if their good taste is their only source of cachet, they don't want to risk losing it by adopting a dud, so they wait to see how things pan out for the innovators and early adopters. The late majority, who are often older and not in step with emerging trends, may not gain awareness of new ideas until they've reached the early majority, but they will typically follow. Lastly, there are the laggards, who may be stubbornly averse to change and only adopt with great reluctance, or who may be detached from society to a degree and thus lacking exposure even to firmly established technologies.

There's one other group, though: non-adopters, who I'd argue could be subdivided into "recusers" and "rejecters." Recusers don't adopt a particular product or technology because they don't feel they need it, or can just as well get by without it. Rejecters may share that sentiment but moreover find the technology to repulse some element of their worldview, and treat their non-adoption as an active protest. For instance, if you ask certain young American urbanites for their opinions on a TV show, a recuser might say, "I haven't seen it" or "I haven't had time to watch it," whereas a rejecter would be more likely to proclaim, with great pride, "I haven't owned a TV for fifteen years."

Non-adopters aren't cave dwellers—they're aware of new technologies, they may even go through the interest and evaluation stages of pre-adoption, but at some point, and it could be anywhere along the adoption curve timeline, they decide that the thing is just not for them. They could be early-stage recusers who give the thing a try and find it falls below their standards, or they could be majority-stage rejecters who see others adopting it and deem it too trendy for their individualistic proclivities. In a way, such rejecters treat rejection as a matter of prestige much like the early adopters value their adoption; the rejecters are simply as bearish on the thing as the adopters are bullish. The crass ones may put a bumper sticker on their car with an image of Calvin from *Calvin and Hobbes* urinating on a Ford logo; the slightly subtler ones might wear a T-shirt with an Apple logo inside a red circle with a diagonal slash across it.

When Beal and Bohlen published their hybrid corn seed adoption studies, they claimed they were only focused on two main ideas that were more or less obvious: that adoption is not a spontaneous decision but rather occurs in stages; and that not everyone adopts at once. In explaining that second idea, they showed how adopters generally share certain characteristics with others who adopt around the same time, and in hindsight this seems to be the actual crux of their report. This is why we study the adoption process: because it's a very organic form of market segmentation. Savvy designers and marketers do well to tailor their offerings as they traverse the adoption curve.

As a researcher, I find that adoption behaviors offer a wonderful lens into the tensions and pressures that people—and societies—face when confronted with something new. For my clients, this lens can also highlight who their next customers could be, how those people will (or won't) make room in their lives for that next thing, and how that thing will reflect on its first owners, its subsequent ones, and even the people who vow never to own it. For all the effort we put into getting an offering out to market, once it hits the shelves, its use, consumption, rejection, or otherwise shapes what it is, what it can be, and ultimately us as well.

Technologies change our bodies: the use of video games and mobile phones have even evolved users' thumbs, and what were once simply handy appendages for holding objects are now the most dexterous digits some people possess. Technologies also change our minds, and what we decide to hold in them: consider the last time you committed a phone number to memory, or did long division. In a paper called "Google Effects on Memory: Cognitive Consequences of Having Information at Our Fingertips," researchers from Columbia, Harvard, and the University of Wisconsin–Madison found that the presence of Internet access lowered people's ability to recall specific information from memory, but increased their ability to recall how and where to access it online. In summing up this so-called Google effect, they suggested that "we have become dependent on [gadgets] to the same degree we are dependent on all the knowledge we gain from our friends and coworkers—and lose if they are out of touch. The experience of losing our Internet connection becomes more and more like losing a friend. We must remain plugged in to know what Google knows," simply because the tools and information for convenience demand it.

These changes are also happening faster than ever before, not necessarily because technology is changing faster, but because our use of it is. The mainstream has quickened its pace of adoption, and abandonment, of today's tools. Increased connectivity—people-to-people, people-to-things, and things-to-things—means that the question of whether to opt into a new technology is increasingly becoming one of whether to opt into or out of the network it occupies, and in the broadest sense, it's a matter of opting into or out of society.

Much as we might imagine our designs in the hands of customers and constituents as ready to be touched and molded to the unique circumstances of their context, they arrive with a set of assumptions of use and acceptable boundaries of use. When technology amplifies existing behaviors, it can be enabling us to remember more, shout farther, or run faster, but we can't assume that the social values surrounding those behaviors will readily change to accommodate the adoption of new technology.

What Beal and Bohlen only hinted at, and what I believe qualitative, in-context research can fundamentally tap into, are the social pressures that contribute to that segmentation, and how those pressures cascade along the curve as adopters exert their influence on those who have yet to adopt. The above paragraph can give you some sense of this cascade, and how both reflective and behavioral design play into its social mechanics, but now let's look a little deeper and see what happens when social pressures grow so strong as to actually change the shape of the adoption curve.

A High-(Peer-)Pressure System on the Horizon

As we saw in the last chapter, the desire to project social status and affirm peer group affiliation can skew behavior in any context, for example, deciding which parts of our conversations we allow others to overhear, or changing one's style of footwear to fit a social group's tastes. But let's examine how it changes the adoption curve in one of the most social-pressure-packed environments: high school.

In 2011 I ran a study in Nigeria, which among many other things is the most populous country in Africa and a rich, if complex, prize for the company that can build market share there. Nigeria, like many countries in Africa, has a relatively young population, with a median age often half that of European or

North American countries,* and technology adoption there reflects both a young and relatively price-sensitive demographic.

Social networks are an inherent part of teenage life the world over, and in Africa arguably even more so because of the young, socially active demographic. When hiring our local team members, we could tell from their profiles that they had a sufficient presence on Facebook. The buzz on the ground in Nigeria around Facebook was palpable, with the cropped, white F in a blue box omnipresent in newspaper articles and advertising for the local operators and mobile phone companies. Being the obvious foreigner in any locale tends to attract some kind of request to connect, and in Nigeria, rightly or wrongly you're perceived as implicitly interesting, wealthy, or a possible business or social connection who may help a person find a better life (the study focused on poorer communities, in which these requests were more prevalent). It used to be that partway through a social exchange a team member was asked for his phone number or email address, but already in Nigeria this had switched to "What's your Facebook?" (The way it was asked, and by whom, suggested that sometimes the asker knew enough to know it was the question to ask, but didn't necessarily have a Facebook account or know enough about the service to sign up and send out friend requests.)

If I asked you for your contact information, what information would you give me? Home or work mailing address? Post office

---

* For example, estimated 2012 figures for median age in years for Egypt (24.9 years), Nigeria (18.4 years), Uganda (15.2), compared with the United Kingdom (41.2), Canada (42.4), or the United States (38.5).

box? One of your email addresses? IM address? Skype? Landline? Mobile phone number? Twitter handle? The answer is dependent in part on why the question is being asked, but all of us have an ever-evolving sense of the connotations that come with each medium: its novelty or its played-outness, its ubiquity or exclusivity, its ease or difficulty of use, and its functional advantages and disadvantages. When someone asks for or offers a point of contact outside your expected worldview, it jars on an emotional level, partly because it suggests that you go out of your way to learn a new process rather than use a known one, and partly because it implies that the world has moved on while you've stayed behind. If at this point you're a Facebook native with a wry smile, be forewarned: your time will come sooner than you think.

That "future shock," as futurist Alvin Toffler once called the psychological effect of "too much change in too short a period of time," is a phenomenon that has existed throughout the lifetime of every living person on earth today, but the dynamics of how this plays out, the speed at which it occurs, and the consequences of adopting or not adopting in the face of it are constantly changing.

Around the same time as I was in Nigeria, I heard a South African parent talk about how over the summer, kids in his son's class switched from Nokia to BlackBerry devices, primarily because of the BlackBerry Messenger (BBM) application, a proprietary instant messaging service available exclusively to BlackBerry users. In a class of thirty students, if the eight most socially active kids are communicating via BBM, do the other twenty-two really have the option of not adopting it? If they didn't have BBM, which conversations would they be part of, which would they miss, and how would their experiences be fundamentally different from their classmates'? What if it's not the eight most influential kids using BBM, but only two? And what if it's only one? At what point does the conversation become confined to that communication channel, and at what point does the decision to opt out of, or reject, that channel become a decision to opt out of a key part of society?

These questions reminded me of the adoption dynamics for mobile phones that I witnessed over the previous decade and a half, where mainstream adopters were pressuring laggards to get their own phones. One such way that pressure played out was that mobile users developed the expectation that they could reach their contacts quickly and at any time of day, wherever they were, and became frustrated when landline-only users couldn't meet that expectation. At a certain point, adult users began buying phones for (typically older) relatives, because the cost of a new phone outweighed the inconvenience of being unable to reach those relatives in any way short of tracking them down in the streets. And all along there were businesses furnishing employees with phones, whether those employees wanted them or not. Regardless of how laggards come to adopt mobile phones or any technology, whenever the pressure builds to the point where laggards are essentially coerced into adoption, it's generally a sign that social norms have shifted and the use of that technology is not just standard but expected.

Yet well before the adoption curve reaches the point where the majority starts to coerce the laggards, social influence plays a significant role in adoption. That influence can come from mass media, but most often it comes from peers. To borrow the old adage about politics, all adoption is local. Well, almost all.

Thomas Valente, currently the director of the University of Southern California's master of public health program, has spent a good portion of his career analyzing social networks and their impact on the diffusion of innovation. In his *Network Models of the Diffusion of Innovations*, he theorized that adoption behavior could be predicted using a threshold model (sound familiar?) of networks. The key factor in adoption, he argued, is the number of one's peers who adopt an innovation; when that number reaches the individual's threshold, that individual will in turn adopt the innovation.

Valente analyzed data from studies on the adoption of the antibiotic tetracycline among American doctors in the 1950s; hybrid corn among Brazilian farmers in the 1960s; and family planning services among married women in South Korea in the 1970s. The data was consistent with Beal and Bohlen's observations that the earliest adopters, the innovators, were the most affected by influences in the greater social system and far less affected by influences within their personal networks. An innovator thus has a very low network threshold, perhaps as low as zero, meaning they may adopt even when none of their peers have done so.

However, beyond the innovators, Valente found that thresholds varied within each adoption category. An early adopter with a high threshold could be exposed to an innovation very early on but wait to adopt until many peers have done so; by contrast, someone else who adopts at the same time, and thus by the classical definition is also considered an early adopter, might find out about the innovation much later but adopt it quickly due to a low threshold. Similarly, a laggard with a low threshold might be what Valente calls an "isolate," someone who simply isn't exposed to the innovation until very late on, while a high-threshold laggard might actually be averse to adoption for a long time, until enough peers have embraced the innovation that the laggard caves in and adopts.

The Valente study provides three important lessons: one, that the adoption curve timeline only tells part of the story, and people who adopt at the same time are not necessarily influenced in the same way; two, that some people, regardless of whether they're early adopters, in the majority, or laggards, are immediately influenced by their peers while others will monitor their peers' behavior for some time before making a decision; and three, that people who may be considered laggards relative to the greater social system could be early adopters within their own personal networks, or vice versa, depending on how their networks are externally connected to the social system. That is to say, you may think your own mom a Luddite, but her friends may look up to her as *très chic*.

So how do these factors play out in the modern age of online social networking? We see that there are fewer isolates: people in Nigeria with Internet connectivity can access roughly the same information about new technologies and trends as people in the United States (although typically at a lower speed), so laggardism tends to be the result of high network thresholds rather than the consequence of living under a rock. (Remember that economic factors limiting consumption are not the same as social factors limiting adoption, at least within the Beal and Bohlen definition as "satisfaction with an idea.")

We also see that the more level informational playing field puts added pressure on the people with low thresholds who want the prestige of being the first among their friends to adopt. They have to adopt increasingly early in order to be the first, but that also means taking risks on innovations that haven't been vetted for usefulness, and sticking with them longer so as not to lose the prestige of being an influencer by backing the wrong horse, hyping it, and then abandoning it. And because more of the innovations being adopted are either connected to online social networks, touted through those networks, or simply are the networks themselves, it's easier to tell who's a laggard, who's a forward-thinking influencer, and who's simply adopting early for early-adoption's sake. Some people will inevitably create new accounts regardless of whether or not they plan to use the service, in order to take (some would say squat) their preferred username, both out of convenience (and inherently inconvenience to others) and because of the assumption that that service will reflect in some way who joined when. When all that activity leaves a digital footprint, the insiders and outsiders, influencers and influencees, become transparent to the whole network.

The Big Picture and the Dirty Little Secret

So far, we've been looking at adoption behaviors on the micro scale: understanding when individuals adopt, what motivates them, how their peers influence them, and how they try to exert influence on their peers. Now let's take this lens and zoom out to the macro level: how a culture can promote or repress adoption; where to look for early adoption on a mass scale to get a sense of how a newer technology might affect an ecosystem; and what challenges innovation faces when attempting to overcome old obstacles. Whenever I'm in the field and want to get some sense of this big picture, I start by looking in a rather unlikely area—the local porn marketplace.

Many people think about sex quite often; some people obsess about it. Reflect for a moment on your own thoughts over the course of today, the people you've met and where you've let your eyes and mind wander. It's no surprise that pornography is a massive industry, estimated at around $14 billion in annual revenue in the United States alone, or about one-third of its bigger and more reputable entertainment-industry brother in Hollywood. Porn is interesting to me in my work because it's what's called "compelling content," in that the demand for it is sufficiently strong to drive the means to consume it. Or to put it another way: porn has the power to drive technology adoption.

There are plenty of other types of compelling content that vary from place to place and person to person—sports scores, weather reports, lifesaving medical information, etc.—and these are all interesting, too, but in my mind they lack the one feature that makes porn compelling to research: it's taboo. The social stigma around porn highlights the concept of "reflective appeal"—just as people are drawn to products that help them show off positive personal traits, they also look for products that can conceal negatively perceived traits. For taboo content such as porn, this tends to force inventive workarounds. This means porn consumers are constantly looking for new, less obvious, and consequently less antisocial ways to consume it. A porn retailer (more often than not set up in an informal market stall) is a good benchmark of the current local standards for content consumption, from Blu-ray to VCD (Video CD, popular in India and parts of Asia) to VHS. The marketplace for porn reveals one culture's connection to others: whether they're importing their porn from the United States, Europe, or Asia, or producing it themselves. It's also worth a look because, frankly, it's much easier to get a sense of consumption there than to strike up a conversation on the street about porn. At least, that's usually the case.

On one of my trips through Old Delhi with a fellow researcher, Younghee Jung, we were invited, as is typical when wandering around markets in India, by a shopkeeper to sit and have a chai. When we got onto the subject of mobile phones, the shopkeeper took out his phone (which happened to be a Nokia, though he didn't know that was the company we worked for) and showed us what was at the time one of the hottest viral videos in India, featuring two seventeen-year-old public school students engaged in oral sex. We were a bit surprised that the shopkeeper would show us the clip, which despite its popularity was still considered quite scandalous (as well as illegal to distribute under Indian law), but even more surprising was the fact that he had the video on his phone despite being relatively tech-illiterate. He explained to us that he had never used Bluetooth before, but he went to the effort of learning how to use the feature specifically in order to get the video onto his phone. He also offered to send the video to us via Bluetooth, if we wanted it, further demonstrating his literacy and his desired standing as an earlier adopter in the network. You're probably familiar with this kind of viral mechanism as it occurs through web-based sharing, but it's important to remember that the spread of technology and media is also constantly playing out offline.

The presence of porn out in public can also reveal broader shifts in cultural norms. On my visit to Kabul in 2008, the DVD stalls on Flower Street were selling Bollywood movies, warlord videos, and the odd action flick. A year later, they were openly selling porn, marking a dramatic shift from the days when the Taliban was so intent on removing the female form from public view that shampoo packaging had female faces scratched out, lest the imagery drive hot-blooded males to distraction. The emergence of an open marketplace for imported pirated porn DVDs could be taken as a sign of a more sexually open mainstream society, and would likely be used by the mullahs as an example of Western decadence. There was no indication of a homegrown porn industry, locally produced content going overseas, or a market for female-consumed or gay and lesbian targeted porn, but such things would be considered even greater indications of permissiveness, as would a shift from an ad hoc marketplace to more established infrastructure, in this case a fixed-location sex shop.*

Checking out the porn market is just one quick-and-dirty way to gauge cultural norms as they relate to the adoption of new technologies and new ideas, and it works well as a supplement to, but not a substitute for, more traditional ethnographic methods. Just as the drivers for porn consumption are universal,

---

* The shift from sex-toy prudence to far more mainstream availability is probably starkest in China, where a decade ago they were out of sight, but today almost every neighborhood has a shop openly selling sex toys and libido enhancers, and penetrative vibrators are sold at the point of sale in convenience stores.

so too are marketplaces for porn. Social norms in countries like Ethiopia or India may push the market out of sight or underground, but they simply force suppliers to find more inventive ways to meet consumer demand. In China, where porn is illegal, some sellers found a subtly ingenious, although admittedly imperfect, way of signaling that their product was for sale: a woman standing at the edge of the market holding a baby wrapped in swaddling. The baby, which was occasionally fake, provided a socially acceptable excuse to stand and talk to the woman, and the porn CDs or DVDs could be hidden in the folds of the cloth.

The lesson from all this is not just that people the world over love porn and are willing to go to great lengths (such as adopting new technologies or pretending to coo over fake babies) to get it. The lesson is that moral codes have a great bearing on adoption, and that you can only understand adoption insofar as you understand the boundaries of moral restrictions, and the choices people make to honor or disobey those boundaries.

Take, for instance, the Amish. The common assumption is that they're rejecters of most forms of technology, because their religious views condemn it, and recusers in other areas where they simply don't need certain technologies in their simple, farm-dwelling lives. However, as Kevin Kelly, who is two steps ahead of most other technology writers and spent time traveling through Amish communities around the United States, and studying their adoption behaviors, reports in his book *What Technology Wants*, "Amish lives are anything but anti-technological. . . . I have found them to be ingenious hackers and tinkers, the ultimate makers and do-it-yourselfers and surprisingly pro technology." Many Amish use power tools in their carpentry work, often excising electric motors and retrofitting the machines to run pneumatically, using diesel generators to power compressed air tanks. Kelly writes that, while every Amish community has its own set of rules, the prevailing attitude toward technology is that it's okay if it helps strengthen the community. But because their traditional ways teach them to remain separate from the rest of society, they thus have to stay off the electricity grid. "The Amish noticed that when their homes were electrified with wires from a generator in town, they became more tied to the rhythms, policies, and concerns of the town. Amish religious belief is founded on the principle that they should remain 'in the world, not of it' and so they should remain separate in as many ways as possible."

The Amish are certainly an outlier among cultures, but the point is that one wrong assumption—that they're hostile toward technology, when really they're just very selective about the technologies they allow into their lifestyle—can completely change outsiders' perceptions of how they really live. The best way to understand how a culture adopts (or doesn't adopt) an innovation is to go there and see it for yourself. In person, you can gain insight into the social barriers unique to a culture, and whether adoption is purely driven by reflective appeal (status), behavioral appeal (usefulness), or the relative importance of one over the other. If you do the research right, it will allow you to tap into the sentiment of adoption, which you'll never get from looking at quantified data.

However, when it comes to cutting-edge technologies that haven't yet been implemented in the community or country you're interested in, it helps to go elsewhere, to the early-adopter places.

They aren't always the most tech-savvy cultures, just the ones that took a particular step first. For next-generation display technologies, Seoul is the place to look. For mobile money services, Kenya provides the dominant model. Tokyo, as discussed at the top of this chapter, is good for looking at highly integrated services across ticketing, noncash payments, and location-based services. "Cutting-edge" can mean many different things when it comes to mobile phone use, and San Francisco, Tokyo, Afghanistan, Ghana, Kenya, and India are all worth a visit to understand their mobile ecosystems. Each provides a sufficient density of people exploring a unique combination of technology and culture in idiosyncratic contexts. Even when the technology stays the same from place to place, the unique nuances of a given location will reveal insights about adoption as you examine how technology has become woven into the fabric of everyday life there.

Of course, by the time you read this, there will be new technologies emerging in unexpected places. The places that are for now ahead of the curve may see the rest of the world catch up to them quickly. As innovations are becoming more and more connected, we are increasingly aware of what people are adopting in other communities. Even the notion of community and human ecosystem is evolving, becoming more social and less tangible, and blurring borders between countries, cultures, and languages.

New Possibilities, New Consequences

Any forward-thinking discussion about the adoption of new technology is bound to be clouded by the natural hopes and fears for an uncertain future. Kevin Kelly adeptly stirred up both ends of that emotional spectrum in *What Technology Wants*, in which he theorized that innovation has an unconscious manifest destiny, a trajectory that we can't control for better and/or for worse. In the context of our recurring theme—technology amplifies existing behavior—the only thing we can truly anticipate is that, eventually, a piece of technology will be adopted by those people who can use it to amplify their behavior the most.

The opportunities, risks, and consequences of adoption greatly depend on the context in which we imagine them playing out. From the modern metropolises of New York and Tokyo to countries with a very different level of risk, such as Afghanistan, I've been exploring how the world will behave when everyone is inherently "known."

What will everyday interactions look like when technology allows you to connect a person standing in front of you to their online profile? There are various ways to do this already: identifying someone by their travel card as they pass through a ticket gate; being tagged by friends in their just-uploaded photos; or a geosocial check-in via Facebook, Foursquare, or some other similar service. At the infrastructural level, personal-data-sharing technologies are already here, but (as of this writing) they have yet to become mainstream through mobile devices, where their impact will be greatest and most visible.

If it all sounds Big Brotherish to you, then good, because by most of today's metrics it is. But it also highlights the privacy tradeoffs we make when we post more of our selves online, driven by a desire to communicate and share our social connections and experiences. While you're worried about what companies and governments are doing with your personal data, you're also propagating that data with ever more detailed tools in the name of socializing or consuming. Keep an eye on Big Brother, but don't forget your socially connected little sister.

One technology already making waves, but for which the biggest disruption is yet to come, is near-time facial recognition: the ability to capture someone's face and accurately match it to their online identity (and everything attached to it), all within the time it takes to say "hi." The technologies required to make this happen are already here but tend to require a big infrastructure—think airports or customs controls. Still, it's only a matter of time before it's available through your mobile phone.

On the streets of Tokyo, advertisers are already using high-tech, camera-equipped billboards that can scan the faces of pedestrians passing by to track their (presumed) gender and age, and use that data to present tailored content. Some might see this as invasive marketing becoming more invasive; others might see it as informational promotion becoming more informative. Either way it's a matter of amplification.

At some point, smartphone users will have access to the same technology. Google has already developed it and decided to withhold it because of privacy concerns, but eventually a developer with a compelling consumer proposition and a different set of ethics will put it out there. While the argument around privacy evokes strong emotions—as it should—recent history suggests that consumers are willing to make privacy tradeoffs for something of value, given the frequency with which smartphone users let companies track their location in return for a blue dot on a map and the lowdown on, say, the nearest four-star pizza parlor. Whether consumers truly understand the long-term impact of those tradeoffs is another thing. I'm sure that there will be compelling facial-recognition applications and services that drive adoption, whether they help people get laid, gossip, or reveal their place in the socioeconomic strata.* People looking to make friends or find mates will have a new resource at their disposal, but so too will those with more nefarious intent.

In 2010 I was running a study in Afghanistan to explore the adoption of M-Paisa, a local mobile money transfer service. The research included a side trip to Jalalabad, on the Pakistan border, which happened to come on the day the U.S. military announced its Iraq exit strategy. In another part of the city, street demonstrations were under way to protest that coalition forces had yet to declare any plans to leave Afghanistan. In any study it's necessary to read the streets, and I know how important it is to let people on the streets read me as well, so I want them to see a friendly guy with a camera casually chatting up the locals. But, hypothetically, if they had had real-time facial recognition at their disposal in that situation, they could have snapped my photo with their phones and instantly seen who I was, where I came from, and whom I worked for.

Want to know whether someone is worth kidnapping? Someday soon, there will be an app for that. On one hand, it's comforting to think they'd have a tool to sniff me out and discover my intent; on the other hand, if they were the type to be

---

* Either through some form of extrapolation of public records—Sweden, Finland, and Norway post this online—or through matching data from salary services with job titles.

suspicious of any foreigner with a corporate background, I wouldn't be able to conceal that connection from them.

This is the paradox of technological evolution: just as it can help us become who we want to be, it can also allow others to expose us for who we really are, for better or for worse.

A Footnote to the Future

There's one last thing to keep in mind when considering how people and societies will adopt the next wave of technologies and the waves to come. When a new innovation enters our consciousness, it's natural to get excited and focus on the uptake of the new—who will adopt, when, and why—and ignore the inevitable slough of the old. But just as all things have an adoption curve, they also have an abandonment curve. There will always be reasons for moving on, and it's simply a matter of when or how they become more compelling than the reasons for staying put: when newer technology makes older ones, such as the phone kiosk, typewriter, and hand-powered drill, effectively obsolete; when society and the nature of work shift, and leave behind things like servants' bells and sword scabbards; or simply because the novelty effect wears off, and Pet Rocks just don't seem as cool anymore. Hints to behaviors past lie all around us: people holding up virtual lighters on their phone screens at concerts; nomenclature like *glove compartment*, *pen pal*, and *disc jockey*; and even the iconography on our computers that points back to the physical objects we've since abandoned in favor of the applications those icons represent—notepads, envelopes, paper clips, and fountain pens. This list may at some point include physical banknotes and coins, physical tickets of any form, metal keys, and the rearview mirror. Just as self-image, relationship networks, social mores, and risk factors all influence the shape and magnitude of adoption curves, so too do they impact abandonment curves. Every wave comes in with the tide, and every tide recedes.

On the flip side of the innovators, early adopters, early majority, late majority, laggards, rejecters, and recusers, there are the dabblers, early abandoners, an early exodus, a late exodus, die-hards, and lifers. Every piece of technology is like a hermit crab's shell, and its users choose to occupy it because it meets their needs at the time they move into it. And just as hermit crabs change shells, people will invariably move on when their needs change or they find something that better suits them.

Chapter 4

You Are What You Carry

I want you to take an inventory, either in your mind or on the nearest available surface, of all the objects that you carried with you when you went out today. Set aside your clothes (which are worn, rather than carried) and start by rummaging around in each of your pockets. Next, open up your wallet, bag, handbag, and/or purse, go through each compartment, and fish out each and every item, including the detritus at the bottom of the bag. For any clusters of things such as keys on a keychain, notes, or receipts, place each one side by side. I want you to take stock in them as individual objects, spread out next to one another, and also appreciate the whole.

Now consider how you came to carry each item with you today, and the journey it took to land in its portable home. Given everything that you own, why did you take only these particular items with you? How much of what you carry is based on decisions you made today, and how much is based on habit? Now, out of all those objects, I want you to choose the items that you wouldn't leave home without, regardless of the day of the week.

If you're an urbanite or suburbanite, the three essential items that you'll have in common with almost every other reader around the world taking this inventory will be keys, money, and a mobile phone. If that seemed like an underwhelming *ta-daaa* moment, it's a testament to the global commonality of how we live and what we value. And if you're not among the vast majority, don't worry: we'll come to the exceptions—which can be just as revealing as the rule—in due course.

What you carry, what you consider essential, and, more important, *why* you carry these things can provide considerable insight into everything from day-to-day activities to hopes, values, beliefs, fears, how people relate to the world around them, and how the world out there relates back to them. For those trying to imagine and build the next wave of products, the subject of why people carry what they carry is fertile ground, touching so many possibilities, especially for those who wish to replace and reinvent those mobile essentials: keys, money, and phone.

On the most basic level, the things we carry, the things we absolutely need when we go out into the world, are the tools that help us survive. In more than a decade of research on this topic, I've found the keys-money-phone triumvirate to be consistent across cultures, gender, economic strata, and age (from teens on up). At their core, all three satisfy our most primal needs. Money can give us access to food and sustenance. Keys provide access to shelter and help keep our things safe while we're away. Mobile phones connect us to each other across space (calling and instant messaging) and across time (texting and email), and as such it is quite possibly the ultimate safety net for a range of emergencies that require connecting to people and things that aren't immediately present. Of course, keys-money-phone offer far more than survival mechanisms, because people always want more than the bare essentials. Most people in the world, even those in relative poverty, live beyond subsistence, and carry more than they necessarily need to simply survive. As you'll see, many other factors, such as status, self-esteem, addiction, and relationships, play an important role, too.

Fundamentally, carrying behavior is about knowing where our belongings are, being able to access them at just the right time, and feeling secure in their safekeeping. When we go out in the world and when we return home, our ability to function depends on security, convenience, reliable solutions, and peace of mind, and these factors motivate us to carry the things we do. We develop habits and strategies to avoid losing things, forgetting them, or having them stolen, and increasingly we're learning how to apply the ways we carry tangible objects toward our intangible, digitally based possessions.

A Place for Everything and Everything in Its Place

My first trip to Shanghai was in 2004. I arrived hellishly jet-lagged after a long haul from Europe, then took a taxi through a polluted winter landscape to a downtown hotel. The team on that trip included a tall blond Swede by the name of Per, and a colleague from a Beijing research laboratory, Liu Ying. Our purpose in China was to explore carrying and interaction behaviors for a client interested in designing carried accessories. Shanghai was the third city in our study, after a month in San Francisco and Berlin, and we were beginning to feel a little frazzled. But we were also deep into the research topic, having spent long days sifting through and starting to make sense of the reams of data that had poured in.

In Shanghai we met a young lady, we'll call her Meili, who had agreed to be one of our in-depth participants, and we were using a research method we refer to as shadowing (also known as "stalking with permission") to tag along in her everyday life and capture her key interactions (and try not to overly influence them with our presence).

As we followed Meili on a shopping trip around the city, from bus to shopping mall, street bench to restaurant, we noticed something interesting about her handbag: it never left her sight. What's more, it never even left her grasp. At no point in the entire day did she set it down, not even while she (awkwardly) tried on a fine new pair of black boots in an upscale shoe store. Every city comes with a risk of theft, but nowhere else in the study, from Milan to Berlin to San Francisco, did we see anyone cling to a bag like that, either holding it in her hand or slinging its strap over her shoulder. It wasn't just that she was keeping it within constant touch, but that it was clasped tight and zipped shut. Or at least when she was conscious of security it was. There was one short moment when, just as she was retrieving something from the bag, she received a phone call that distracted her from the task and caused her to leave the bag open and unzipped for a minute or two. When she realized this, she was visibly upset with herself that she had let her guard down for even a moment.

It might seem like extreme caution, although not unwarranted, since the risk of theft in Shanghai is a good deal higher than in most metropolises around the world. However, it got our research team thinking: don't we all act like that to some degree? We don't all clutch our bags at all times, but how often have you been in a dimly lit bar and slid yours under a chair to keep it close? Conversely, have you ever been in a friendly neighborhood café and felt comfortable enough to leave your belongings in the care of strangers while you popped into the restroom?

We termed this phenomenon the *range of distribution*, the distance that people are willing to let physical objects stray when they're out and about. The criteria people use to make these decisions (whether consciously or not) are simple, and fairly universal: the perceived risk of danger, the actual risk of danger, and the perceived and actual need to keep items close at hand for convenience. When risk and convenience factors are low, objects are allowed to spread out; when convenience is high, they stay close by; when risk is high, they stay somewhere safe, which could be very close, very deep under lock and key, or even somewhere completely intangible (we'll come back to that last one later).

Range of distribution is a particularly useful lens in contextual research, as it can provide perspective on the perception of risk of both the environment and the individuals in it. On public transit in China and Brazil you'll often see riders wearing backpacks on their chests (or "frontpacks"), a strong indicator of a short range of distribution, a high risk of theft, and an acute awareness of that risk and the need to react quickly if errant hands start unzipping a pocket.

On occasion, the local infrastructure can force this behavior. When the Shanghai Metro introduced (airport-style) X-ray bag scanners in advance of Expo 2010 (the Shanghai World's Fair), I noticed an accompanying change in behavior among mainstream passengers, and their anxiety, particularly during rush hour, was evident. As they placed their bags on the conveyor, many passengers desperately maintained eye (and sometimes hand) contact with their possessions, as if the conveyor belt would suddenly cause a break in the space-time continuum and whisk their valuables to another dimension. As soon as bags crossed the apparent threshold of no return, the passengers' attention and behavior would rapidly shift to the outgoing end of the machine, where they waited to grab their own bags the instant they emerged. If a passenger let his attention lapse for even a moment, he ran the risk that someone else would whisk his bag away and disappear into the rush-hour throng (if the space-time gremlins didn't get hold of it first).

The optimal or acceptable range of distribution depends on a number of contextual factors, including the physical properties of the space; familiarity with that space; the presence of familiar people (including people we recognize but haven't yet spoken to); the density of strangers; what activities people are engaged in nearby; the general cleanliness of the space and the people in it; the types of objects distributed, their actual value, and the owner's perceptions of their theft-worthiness; the time of day; visibility; weather; and so on. This equation tends to create certain sets of well-understood, if unarticulated, norms for particular contexts, like the "frontpack" on Chinese and Brazilian public transit. Individuals who behave counter to prevailing norms tend to stand out. If the gap is broad, we might take the outlier's behavior as a sign of paranoia, or a lack of contextual awareness (one of the reasons why tourists tend to be more obvious targets of theft, and why frequent travelers look to locals for cues to blend in), but it could also be an indication of the owner's sense of an object's value. A wallet full of one-dollar bills doesn't look any different on the outside than a wallet full of hundred-dollar bills, but they'll probably have different ranges of distribution.

We've all been in group situations where one person casually displays an object with the obvious intention to impress: using a car key fob to steer a conversation toward a new car; letting a particular (or particularly expensive) brand label slip into view; calculatedly pulling out the latest and greatest smartphone to check for messages. Maybe you consciously do it, too—in subtle or not-so-subtle ways. The ability to project status in the form of tangible objects depends on their (momentary, at the very least) visibility but also highlights an inherent tension: the desire to show off one's property versus the desire to keep it safe. The high visibility and symbolic value that at one point made Apple's white earbud headphones so popular (as discussed in chapter 2) are also significant drivers for theft. Thus, deciding on a comfortable range of distribution for a status object requires a trade-off: project it or protect it.

In the home, where risks to possessions are relatively minimal and convenience is paramount, we tend to distribute things in the places we'll need them, or where we'll know we can find them when we need them. Just as most people put their food close to where they cook and their toilet paper within arm's length of the toilet, things people carry into the outside world (coats, bags, keys, etc.) tend to linger around the front or back door. For most adults, mobile phones usually gravitate to the edge of a desk, and for teens these objects are left closer to the bed—both preferably within a cord's distance of a power supply.

We call these places where portable objects tend to cluster *centers of gravity*. A center of gravity is the bull's-eye where we aim to set an object down and the first place we look to retrieve it. Their purpose is fairly obvious: they are our spatial mnemonic devices. People who keep keys on hooks by the door are unlikely to lose their keys. People who keep cash, ID cards, credit cards, public transit fare cards, library cards, business cards, and such in their wallets, which they keep in their pockets, don't have to think twice when they need to access any of those things. In terms of range of distribution, centers of gravity are signs that mental convenience can be just as important as physical convenience.

But even the act of clustering objects in places where we are more likely to find them is no guarantee that we'll remember to take them with us, or keep them within an ideal range of distribution. When our awareness is impaired, whether we're busy, tired, drunk, or daydreaming, objects quickly become ostensibly invisible, and thus forgotten. To counter this natural tendency to forget important objects, one of the simple, widespread behaviors people exhibit when leaving one space and heading to another is what we call a *point of reflection*, that moment when a person pauses in order to run through a mental checklist of what they're carrying and what they may be forgetting. For someone leaving home, this usually includes the essentials—keys,

money (or the wallet/purse containing it), and mobile phone—
and whatever travel items the day calls for. In a highly ritualized
motion, we pat pockets and look in bags to reaffirm these objects' persistence before walking out the door, stepping out of
the car, leaving the work desk, or getting up from a restaurant
table. Some people even recite the checklist aloud.

That little pause at a point of reflection is such a simple,
mundane behavior that it may not scream "business opportunity," but the potential is certainly there, if perhaps at whisper
volume. The idea of periodic, systematic reminders based on
context and necessity is one that can extend to problems and
needs far beyond physical objects.

It's easy to tell if your phone is in your pocket when you can
feel it; however, it's impossible to discern how much credit you
have left on your fare card just by touching or looking at it (unless the amount is printed on its surface). One of the reasons
why wallet mapping is such a useful research technique—
literally sifting through and documenting the contents of
people's wallets and/or bags, and asking about the stories behind
each object—is that people often do things to compensate when
things like fare cards aren't designed with adequate points of
reflection. The most common form of compensation is redundancy: if you don't know how much credit is on your primary
fare card, carry a backup that you know will have enough to get
you through the turnstiles when you're in a hurry and you spot
your train pulling into the station.

From a service design perspective, such a redundancy means
there's an opportunity to make the system more efficient. For
instance, most vending machines in Tokyo, and not just in metro

stations, have a mechanism that allows anyone to check their fare card balance just by swiping it against that machine—a very intentional and well-thought-out point of reflection, and it doesn't require a purchase. This simple interaction is both intuitive and useful, allowing people to use infrastructure in the world around them to query the status of their belongings.

Pocket-taps and habitual pauses by the door will always be easy ways to check up on physical objects, just as key hooks and tight grips on handbags will help us keep track of those things. But as more and more of our possessions become digitized, we have to reexamine these fundamentals of carrying behavior—ranges of distribution, centers of gravity, and points of reflection—in terms of their intangible equivalents. With change comes opportunity.

You Are What You Upload

When Apple released the first iPod in 2001, they touted it as "1,000 songs in your pocket." By 2009, that figure was up to 40,000 songs. But by 2011, the new promise was . . . zero.

Sure, if you wanted to do things the old-fashioned way you could still store thousands of songs on the device's hard drive, but you could just as well keep your entire music library on Apple's servers and stream them through iCloud, freeing up plenty of memory for all your different versions of Angry Birds.

Just as smartphones have changed the notion of the phone from a two-way communication terminal into a gateway to the world's knowledge base (it's never been easier to look up Liberace's birthday while riding the bus), server-based storage systems like the cloud offer the promise of revolutionizing how we transport our own digital belongings. Rosy as its near-limitless capacity and whenever-wherever-access value propositions may seem, cloud-based offerings still have to contend with the challenges of providing security, convenience, reliability, and peace of mind— the underlying drivers that create carrying behaviors like range of distribution, centers of gravity, and points of reflection.

It's easy to see how digitization and cloud storage represent a lightening of our physical loads—a Great Unburdening, if you will. Imagine going back to the twentieth century and trying to carry everything you can now store (and, equally important, access) on a smartphone, laptop, tablet, or e-reader. Walking out the door in the morning, you'd be towing along one set of shelves with every CD, cassette, and LP in your music collection (if you're carrying the equivalent of an on-demand music streaming service like Spotify, your shelves might number in the millions); another set of shelves with all your books, including a twenty-nine-volume *Encyclopaedia Britannica* set and a twenty-volume *Oxford English Dictionary* set; a third with all your photo albums; and a shoe box full of all the letters you'd sent and received over the past year, as well as bills and bank statements, and every map of every part of the world at every scale. If you wanted entertainment, you might even bring a few movies—and your TV set and VCR or DVD player. Leaving work in the evening, you'd not only be hauling all that back home, you'd also have your four-foot-high metal filing cabinet, Rolodex, and in/out memo tray. Factor in the tangible equivalent of Internet access and you'd be lugging around several Libraries of Congress. On top of all that, you'd be carrying quite a few things you probably never owned before, like a weather station that collects data from every corner of the world and a compendium of the opinions of millions of strangers on everything from restaurants to manga. Not only would you have one hell of a sore back, but you'd also be quite hard-pressed to keep an eye on everything as you towed it about town.

Now, just because you can easily fit all those things in your pocket doesn't mean you constantly need them when you're on the go, or can even keep track of them well enough to access them when you do need them. And simply because you can reduce them to bytes doesn't mean you're ready to get rid of their tangible forms. One faulty hard drive, hacked server, or unpaid cloud-storage bill and you could lose everything if it's not backed up elsewhere. Plus, that convenient bundle of personal material and work material folded together into one travel-size container can easily muddle the boundaries between the two. While the Great Unburdening is indisputable on a physical level, the psychological tradeoffs associated with going to zero have far more challenges, but just as much potential.

Consider the things that impact the range of distribution, how closely we hold our belongings or allow them to stray, in terms of both physical distance and level of consciousness, as a yo-yo. How long can we comfortably let its string go out and still be able to snap it back when we need it in hand? And how fast can we snap it back?

When things become digital, the range of distribution equation changes. Those yo-yo strings can be much longer, in terms of physical distance (retrieving a document saved on a computer or server far, far away), time distance (retrieving an email you sent a year ago), and distance from consciousness (listening to a song you hadn't heard in years until your randomized playlist decided to play it). A long string on a tangible object makes it much harder to snap back, at the very least requiring you to expend time moving from point A to point B and then back to A to retrieve the object. But if it's digital, you can snap it back incredibly quickly even if you don't know where it is, as long as you have the option of a reliable search function. Going digital means you can juggle many more strings at once, crisscross them in myriad ways (for example, embed a video in a slideshow presentation, attach a photo to an email), and, like a cat's cradle, create collaborative networks of strings between multiple users. It even allows you to cut some of the tangible-object strings and still snap those objects back later by creating perfect reproductions on demand; in the past this has meant burning CDs, but in the future it will mean 3-D printing. Forget to pack your dentures for a trip? No problem, just call ahead to the hotel and have them find a local dentist to 3-D print a duplicate set that will be ready for you when you arrive.

Technological advances may also change our need to measure out those yo-yo strings. We might think of range of distribution as a "sixth sense" for certain people in certain situations, like a parent walking through a busy shopping mall with a small child, but less instinctual when carrying less valuable (and not so irreplaceable) items. However, the desire to maintain preternatural awareness for the purpose of avoiding loss and theft is still strong enough to make this area ripe for disruption, especially as the means to track things grow ever more sophisticated.

In the summer of 2012, I accidently left that most eminently connected device of the time—an iPhone—in a taxi in Shanghai.

Upon returning home, I used an online find-my-device service to track it as it bounced around the city. I'd already put in a call to the taxi company, which their controller routed to the driver (whose contact information appeared on the receipt), who denied it was in his taxi, despite the fact that I could pinpoint its location, speed, and direction it was heading, and despite the loud alerts I kept piping through to the itinerant phone itself. Watching hundreds of dollars' worth of personal gear zigzag, come to a halt, double back, and at some point pass within blocks of my apartment was quite mesmerizing, though it heightened the frustration of never getting it back.

Although I had mislaid the phone, it wasn't lost in the sense of sitting in an unknown location, but rather that it was simply out of reach. Part of my assumption about its ultimate loss was that it had a (gray-market resale) value that exceeded any social obligation to return it, a bonus equivalent to a few days' wages for a Chinese taxi driver, with perhaps a small cut for the controller. And just to be clear, I'm not begrudging him for keeping the phone, as I would expect taxi drivers in most countries to do the same.* But it is a fine example of a near-term look at what "losing" something will mean over time as technology allows much of what we own to communicate its location, either as GPS-embedded objects like cars, bicycles, remote controls, and jewelry, or because we are inherently recording much more of

---

* In fact, one side experiment I conducted explored the honesty of random strangers by giving them cash and asking them to hand it to a third party (previously unknown to the participant). Six out of ten lots of money ended up being passed on—far more than initially hypothesized.

the world around us and can ascertain from this data where something is.

In the future, connected devices may include a return-to-sender feature—an incentivized reward for a stranger who moves an object from a place where the object would be considered "lost" to one where it would be "found," or retrievable. To extrapolate, this traceability would theoretically change our sense of what it means to own something, if the consequences of misplacing it are diminished and the ease of retrieval heightened. Most people might prefer to have a lost object returned, but what if it had its value automatically calculated and was then offered for sale to the finder, or claimable by the highest nearby bidder? Some would lament reducing the world to sentimental-valueless numbers, but others might build a lifestyle around buying and selling rights to use if not ownership itself.

The power of location-based mobile data adds yet another dimension to the range of distribution: just-in-time decision-making. Not only does it allow us to forgo things like paper maps in favor of far less clunky digital ones; it also allows us to venture out in the world with a near-total lack of awareness of what we're going to do, and trust that our mobile device will connect us to the things that are important to us. Instead of planning routes, we can rely on GPS; instead of planning a night on the town, we can walk out the door, check Foursquare to see what our friends or our friends' friends have done and are doing, and base our decision on that; instead of arranging meeting times and places, we can agree on a general part of town and microcoordinate via calls and messages to get closer and closer until we find one another. Those yo-yo strings that connect us to people and things can be infinitely long—so long that we can allow ourselves to lose conscious awareness of the things on the other ends—and yet we can snap them back instantaneously whenever we want (provided the network cooperates).

We can even take things a step further from consciousness and delegate the snap-back to automated systems. It's something we already do in the form of reminders and alerts through our phones' calendars and services like Mint.com. As a thought exercise, let's look at an example mentioned briefly when we were contemplating the future of thresholds: predictive shipping.

Let's say a company, like Amazon, that uses algorithms to analyze and predict its customers' shopping habits develops those algorithms to such a point that they can ship products that haven't even been ordered. They're so confident that the customer will want or need those products that they're willing to eat the costs if they're wrong. Let's say you love travel, and you affiliate yourself with a brand like *Condé Nast Traveler*. One morning you open your front door to find *Condé Nast Traveler*'s ultimate travel shirt, in your size, in the style of a magazine shoot that you lingered on for a few minutes yesterday, on your doorstep. From your past purchasing behavior, they've seen that you've worn similar shirts and bought some pants and accessories that would match this shirt. They know what style you like by analyzing your peer group and your fashion adoption habits via social media, and they know you trust the tastemakers at *Condé Nast Traveler* to bring you something that is not only relevant to you but also relevant to the culture you engage in.

If Amazon's analysis proves correct and you decide to wear the shirt, it could relay back to them that you've worn it and automatically debit your credit card. If you decide not to keep the shirt, simply put it back in the box, leave it outside your door, and let Amazon do the rest. With similar nodes, Amazon could even monitor your supplies of groceries or toilet paper and ship you fresh stock before you run out.

Too many false positives and this is the worst form of junk mail, and the much higher up-front cost of delivery would ultimately make the business model unviable. But for certain products, brands, and demographics, it could work. Where is there intense brand loyalty and incredible insight into the lives of consumers, including their offline and/or online window-shopping? In one sense we already have this with subscription services: if you get a newspaper delivered to your doorstep every day, you don't know if it will always have desirable content, but you know enough about it (and the paper knows enough about you and its other readers) that you willingly pay for it. Of course there are issues around privacy invasion, homogeneous consumption, and irregular behaviors that algorithms don't quite understand, but it's just one possible trajectory to get you thinking about how the possibilities of technological advancement could create a new kind of marketplace for predictive products.

Such a service might not seem like it has much to do with carrying behavior, other than saving consumers from carrying shopping bags home from stores. But it actually gets at the very essence of carrying behavior: having things at hand when we need them, where we need them, and using memory and proximity to keep track of them. What would it take for Amazon to know that you forgot to pack a swimsuit for your trip to the Bahamas, and for them to have a new one in your size and style waiting for you at the hotel before you got there or even had a chance to realize your mistake? It could simply be a matter of putting a few tags and sensors on your clothes and suitcase, asking you a few questions about your travel behavior, and programming some basic automation.

Imagine walking into your home after a long day at work, only to encounter one of the strangest sights you've ever seen. While you were out, someone flipped an antigravity switch in your home, and as you float through the door you see your kitchen sink and your nightstand drift past, side by side. Your rug is on the wall; your dog is on the ceiling. Nothing has left the house, but it still feels like everything is lost.

Would it freak you out? The craziest thing about that scenario is that it's one we can't seem to easily avoid and must face constantly—albeit in the digital realm. Where do people expect to find their online things? And what knowledge do they need to retrieve them? Without a framework that cues us to where things should sit and how to access them, we're all a bunch of Major Toms floating in the digital ether. A good interface makes a world of difference, but search functionality can also create ad hoc centers of gravity. What if, in the spirit of the Great Unburdening, a system was designed to create these centers of gravity ahead of time and unburden the user from the search? Say you have a meeting coming up about a particular project; if the system knows about it in advance, and understands how you typically access files before or during a meeting, it can cluster them for you and preload them onto your phone or computer so they're there when you need them.

In the same spirit, there are opportunities to design digital points of reflection, when the system knows what you're forgetting before you forget it. Gmail has done this already: if you put the word *attach*, or any variation of it, into the body of an email without attaching a file, Gmail asks if you want to attach a file before sending.

Of course, the easiest way to never forget anything is to never have anything to remember.

Why Carry Anything?

Afghanistan can be a chaotic place by any measure, but its perils don't always come in the form of bombs and kidnappings. In urban areas, the risk of theft is almost always present, and you could say the country as a whole has a relatively tight range of distribution. But theft isn't always about what's being taken from your pockets: it's also about what's not being put into them.

In 2010, mobile telecom provider Roshan and the Afghan Ministry of the Interior set up a pilot program to explore paying police officers' salaries via a mobile banking system called M-Paisa.* Instead of receiving bundles of cash from their commanding officers, the police who participated in the M-Paisa program were notified by text message that their salaries had been credited to

---

* The Roshan M-Paisa in Afghanistan and the Vodacom M-Pesa in Kenya are variations of the same thing; the difference in spelling is deliberate.

their accounts, which they could cash out through any Roshan agent in the country.

To their surprise, many officers found that they had received "raises"—sometimes as much as a third more than they were accustomed to getting. In fact, they were getting their full, actual salaries for the first time, as the money digitally slipped through the sticky fingers of the higher-ups who had been skimming off the top.

On the surface, it seems like a very positive story with a happy ending: less graft, a more efficient payroll system, and everyone's happy except for the corrupt middlemen (one of whom was so upset about the new system that he rounded up all of his underlings' SIM cards so he could collect the money himself; a Roshan employee reported the commander to the Ministry of the Interior, who didn't prosecute him but promptly put an end to his scheme).

However, the upshot was a bit more complicated. You'd think that, aside from the "bonus" money, the police officers who were paid through M-Paisa would enjoy the benefit of an account that safeguarded their money from pickpockets as well as corrupt bosses. But the range-of-distribution culture in Afghanistan, coupled with low levels of financial and technological literacy (only 9 percent of Afghanis have accounts at formal financial institutions), creates a paradox: the perceived risk of theft is so high that tangibility is believed to be the only form of security—if you can't see it, you don't own it.

Most officers in the program reported cashing out immediately after receiving notice of deposits. Some had to travel to neighboring towns because the Roshan agents near them had opted out of the M-Paisa program due to fears of being robbed of their cash reserves. In Taliban strongholds, agents reported threats of attacks from militants who saw M-Paisa and mobile phones in general as heretical tools of Westernization.

The context of war, poverty, and high rates of illiteracy (on multiple levels) makes Afghanistan an extreme example for many behaviors, not just those around money carrying, but a valuable case study nonetheless. We already live in a world where mobile phones allow us to carry more tools while carrying fewer objects, and we can easily imagine a future where everything that goes into a wallet can be converted into digital forms that we access through a single electronic device. But is that a realistic future? And will people be happy with it?

As it stands, that isn't the future. People are risk-averse, and when you look at what they carry today and the redundancies that exist, it becomes clear that people carry more than the bare minimum because they feel most comfortable when provisioning for contingencies. It might not be efficient to carry cash, a cash card, and two credit cards, but the consequences of a nonfunctioning cash card are severe enough to make the safety net worthwhile. There's no precise formula to determine what combination of risk probability and consequence cost creates contingency provisioning, but this is yet another aspect of life where behavior changes when a threshold is reached.

If our goal is to lighten consumers' loads and help them be more efficient with what they carry, we could try to either reduce the risk of losing things, reduce the cost of recovering or replacing those things, and/or make it easier to live without carrying those things around. One of the simplest ways to accomplish all three is to allow people to use more while owning less.

Entrepreneur and author Lisa Gansky calls this "the Mesh," a model for consumption based on network-enabled sharing, providing access rather than ownership. One of the more famous examples of a Mesh business is Zipcar, the membership-based car-sharing network, which distributes cars around cities and college campuses for people who don't own a car but occasionally need to use one. Public libraries fit the model, too, sans profit. Other networks have cropped up in recent years, thanks to the Internet, providing both public and private goods for temporary use, from tool-lending libraries to children's toy rental services.

Such systems work because of the power of networks, and the ability to access the goods as nodes in the network. For instance, a Zipcar user can search online for a car stationed nearby, reserve it, and then unlock it with a membership card; the doors will open only for the user designated to have access at that time.

As more of what we carry becomes digital and networkable (or includes networked components), and as we develop identification systems to allow us secure access and payment to the network, we will see radically different ways of interacting with and using goods. Theoretically, we could go to a "superdistribution" model, like Zipcar but without the reservations or the cards. Goods could be scattered around a city in areas where they're likely to be accessed; when someone picks up an object to use it, the object identifies its user biometrically and automatically bills for the duration of access. If it's easy enough to find and use a laptop while you're out and about in the city, why carry your own around? And if the laptop can identify you, and identify anyone who tries to pluck it from your grasp, why worry about the risk of theft? There's no way to steal something that has no owner.

A Whole New World Outside Your Door

As we've seen, mobile technology has dramatically changed people's behaviors outside the home, from carrying less to remembering less to owning less. All sorts of things have become possible. It feels like a major advancement just to have a digital map instead of a paper one in a place like Los Angeles; in parts of the world like Uganda it's a major leap forward when a mother with a very sick child can use a mobile phone to find the nearest doctor and not have to worry about carrying her child ten miles to the nearest town only to discover there's no doctor there.

This evolution is certainly not without perils, from the annoyance of losing one's phone to the collective suffering caused by a major system failure or a security breach. We're still learning what it means to be at the mercy of the network; in my own experience, network disconnections have resulted in everything from the minor irritation of losing a phone signal in the canyons of Manhattan to the challenge of being stuck at a hotel in Tanzania with a nonworking credit card and no other form of payment.

Even though we can't entirely trust networks, we still put plenty of faith in them because they can—and increasingly will—do for us what we can't do for ourselves, or at least can't remember to do. Over the next few years we're likely to see more points of reflection designed into objects that are increasingly connected to one another. In Tokyo today you can walk up to vending machines and, before you decide to spend your last few hundred yen on a soda, place your wallet against a sensor that will read your Suica card and tell you if you have enough credit left on it to take the train home or buy the soda, or both.

As networks and infrastructure get smarter and faster, we'll also see our notions of convenience change; instead of paying for the convenience of having the right atoms and molecules in the right place at the right time, we now pay to have the right bits and bytes where and when we want them. This means more data portals in more places, but it also means more everyday objects that we can interact with, and that can understand us and interact back. Perhaps all those objects will become connected through a public, networked infrastructure, where anyone can walk up to any node of the network, be recognized by the network, and have access approved and initiated within seconds. What would it take to create that? Is it even feasible? I can't say, but it's a possibility that bears considering when we think about the future of how people will carry and use objects outside their homes.

In some ways, we're already in that future, though it's easy at times to take for granted what it really means to be connected when we're out there. Sometimes the best way to get a sense of our networked selves is to see what happens when we get off the grid.

During the Arab Spring in 2011, I had the opportunity to conduct a study in Egypt. Many of the news reports out of Cairo during the weeks of tension had made a big deal of the protesters' use of social media, and although I was skeptical of the dimensions of its impact as they were reported outside the country, it was clear that access to mobile technology and an active network had reshaped the nature of survival and communication during a conflict.

As a researcher, information access is always critical for me to do my work, and I wanted to explore what it would be like to lose the on-the-go resources I'm accustomed to. At the time, Libya's civil war was still raging, and many communications channels had been cut. A colleague and I wanted to get a light sense of the situation there—the "rebels" had hacked into and were piggybacking onto the state mobile phone network, making for an interesting tech angle—so we negotiated with a taxi driver in Cairo to take us over. Eight hours later, we were ready to cross the border.

Immediately upon crossing into Libya, we lost our cell connectivity, which meant losing our entire support structure—maps, email, phone, web access—and with it the ability to call for help, to locate ourselves and the nearest town, to translate without interpreters. Losing those lifelines left us feeling naked, more exposed to the dangers you would associate with a border town in a time of conflict, but it also forced us to heighten our awareness of where we were at every moment, where we had come from, and how to get back there.

We're very fortunate to live in a world where we can go almost anywhere (though certainly not everywhere, at least for now) with tremendously powerful tools for communication and information that fit inside our pockets and bags. They are our tools for survival, but it's important to remember that both our tools and our ideas about what "survival" means are constantly evolving. The more we come to understand the latter, the better equipped we'll be to harness technology and create tools that really matter.

Chapter 5

Calibrating Your
Cultural Compass

When you want to know how and why people do the things they do, the best people to learn from are the doers themselves, and the best place to learn is where the doing gets done. This is the simple premise of design research. It's a state of mind as much as it is a practice, and it holds whether you're by yourself for an hour or have a team of five people working with you for a month. The more experience you have, the more likely it is that you can find something that shapes the way you and others think and ultimately changes your and their courses of action.

In an increasingly connected world there's a temptation to think that a nuanced understanding of people and places can be found online, through social media accounts, self-documentation, street views, and a number of services that put a stream of data out there—where consumers are, what they are listening to, what brands they like, and so on. But these are only the crumbs on the surface of the rich, deep, multilayered casserole of human experience, and the only way to slice straight through it is to travel and be *in it*. "Going native" is hardly the exclusive domain of anthropologists. Although they have the luxury of spending weeks, months, or even years getting acclimated to a new culture, even the briefest dip in the contextual-awareness pool can yield insights and inspiration.

In previous chapters I've highlighted new ways of understanding behavior through the lenses of several broad social constructs and the technologies that facilitate or impede them. Now I'd like to shift focus to the context in which these forces are at play—not just *how* to look, but *where* to look. Over the course of this chapter I'll outline a handful of techniques for conducting what I call "rapid cultural calibration"—not only putting yourself in the local mind-set but also putting local phenomena into global perspective, implicitly and sometimes explicitly. I frequently use these techniques to give team members a sound basis for understanding the more stringent data they collect via formal research.

Rapid cultural calibration can take the form of a stroll at dawn or a rush-hour subway ride; a visit to a barbershop, a train station, or the local outpost of a global chain restaurant; or even a slight pause for contemplation at the sight of signage. Used in conjunction with more structured techniques such as in-depth interviews, surveys, and home visits—and when applied in multiple neighborhoods, cities, or countries—rapid cultural calibration can help deepen your understanding of a new culture and compare it with your own and others you've visited. Each calibration session can take as little as thirty minutes, or stretch as long as half a day (though if you were so inclined, you could do them ad infinitum, but in that case they wouldn't be particularly rapid).

Waking Up with the City

Across the globe, the best time to observe a city is around the crack of dawn and the hours that follow. It's not that the afternoon or night doesn't reveal things that can't be found at other times, but that the start of the day tends to be more consistent and more regimented than the day's end. For those of us trying to soak up local nuances, it's easier to observe more people in a shorter space of time as the city finds its rhythm to the tune of the morning commute.

Every city and season is slightly different, but the "waking up with the city" exercise typically starts around 4 a.m.* on a weekday. The ideal neighborhood is walkable, includes a mix of both residential and retail spaces, and broadly reflects the types of demographic target of the study in question. These trips work best when local team members can pair up with the visiting team to discuss observations from a cross-cultural vantage point. Sometimes it takes a bleary-eyed rickshaw, taxi, tuk-tuk, boda-boda, or bicycle ride to transport the team to the right part of town.

Over the course of the morning, the neighborhoods slowly reveal themselves. This often starts with the infrastructural support: shop deliveries, road sweepers, repair, waste disposal, and any other services that need to be taken care of before the

---

* The 5–7 a.m. slot is particularly good for cruising dodgy neighborhoods where the people who pose the highest risk to the team are either asleep or too wasted to care, and because the less violent members of society are starting to go about their business, mitigating the risk of aggression.

influx of pedestrian and vehicular traffic makes these tasks more difficult. A simple operation like waste collection can reveal patterns of behavior that occur inside the home. In cities like Tokyo and Seoul there are discrete days for recycling materials such as tins, cardboard, plastics, and organic materials, and there is significant social pressure to conform to the rules of what items are put where and when. This presorted recycling provides a window into what products people are consuming in a given area and a ringside view of electronics recycling, since these require a special permit and are placed to one side. In parts of London and San Francisco, it's generally fine for larger furniture such as chairs, cupboards, or beds to be placed by the curb, on the assumption that someone on the street will come along and claim it. Compare this with Old Delhi, where a rudimentary bed frame on the street might be used where it lies, still occupied by its sleeper(s) in the early hours.

In residential areas, you'll find locals engaged in their pre-work activities of choice. In a city like Tokyo, this often includes joggers in running regalia and large-dog walkers (smaller dogs are far more visible in the city at other parts of the day, and tend to be exercised in closer proximity to homes). In New Delhi, the local equivalent is power walkers and joggers who congregate in small patches of park dressed in what most nonlocals would assume is office attire (at least for men—slacks and a shirt, with sneakers being the tip of the hat to Western notions of appropriate exercise gear), and where the only dogs will be strays on the street. A second-tier Chinese city such as Hangzhou takes a very different tack, with local exercise very much geared around bringing the local elderly community out into public squares and other spaces for group exercise activities, ranging from tai chi to ballroom dancing—all to sounds emanating from car-battery-powered mobile speakers. By 6 a.m. in Bangkok you will have already missed the hard-core athletes who use the coolest hours of the night for training.

In the hours before retail businesses open, you might notice how people and businesses in the community protect themselves overnight with, for instance, shutters and locks—conventions that might give you some sense of how this particular neighborhood deals with threats of vandalism or theft. And, of course, the absence of such conventions can be just as enlightening.

Some businesses open with a bang, while others, particularly those whose owners and employees have more local connections to the community, come to life more slowly. Even while the lights warm up and the "closed" signs remain unflipped, a local baker's shop in London might keep the door wedged open for ventilation and serve a loyal customer who pops his head around the door, a practice that speaks to established relationships and situations in which rules (opening and closing times) are broken and by whom. That may be contrasted elsewhere by the all-or-nothing rattle of a chain store grill being pulled up to announce that they are officially open. These simple rituals offer a sense of the strength of social and commercial relationships.

As the morning unfolds, the street starts to bustle with more energy and more people. You get to watch the first wave of commuters leave their homes and start the trek across the city to their jobs. You see how kids get to school, whether they wear uniforms, and whether they travel alone, in groups, or with a parent. All of these details say a lot about levels of trust in a neighborhood or city. You also get a glimpse of breakfasting behaviors: what foods people line up for, what kinds of people eat on the street, and whether they eat in a fixed place or on the go. Morning markets are far more vibrant than ones later in the day.

By 8 or 9 a.m., you should have a much better sense of how the city starts its day than you'll ever be able to gather in your hotel's lobby (although there's much to be said for people-watching there, too). At this juncture, I like to bring the whole team together for a recap over breakfast of ginger tea, congee, bacon rolls, or whatever the locale serves up, before heading back to our accommodation to rest up a bit before heading out for the rest of the day's research.

Ride Local

You can never understand the stresses and pains a city's inhabitants feel until you've felt the worst of its commute. The demands of punctuality pack more pressure into morning commutes than evening ones, thus magnifying the impact of any obstacles that crop up along the way. London favors the expensive-slow-and-unreliable commute. Cairo does it packed-noisy-and-hot. Tokyo's efficiency is on par with its density, and if you're lucky enough to join the Keio Line into Shinjuku Station during rush hour in the rainy season you can appreciate the spatial dynamics, texture, and scent of a sardine can. In Tokyo, if a commuter train is delayed by more than a few minutes, late notes are handed out to commuters to present to their office, evidence of both the infrequency of this event and the traditionally hierarchical nature of authority in companies. And Bangkok, despite the very effective MRT (Metropolitan Rapid Transit) cruising over the city, still does a mean gridlock.

In Los Angeles, car commuters time their slog to work against the telltale red lines on their in-car navigation systems. In Beijing, this story has evolved: everyone knows that the entire city will be covered in red lines for a certain duration, and they simply plan their drive to include work activities such as scheduling important calls. It turns out being able to plan ahead for a predictable commuter experience is a big part of quality of life, even if it means planning ahead for sitting in traffic.

What are the modes of transport people use to get from where they live to where they study or work? What are the environmental conditions—heat, humidity, and density? How smooth is the ride? How even is the road? What is the likelihood of being able to sit versus being forced to stand? What kinds of activities does that space afford at each stage of the journey? How much does it cost, and how do people pay? What activities are considered acceptable and unacceptable in each space?

These are the sorts of questions that come up when our teams venture into the melee of the daily commute, and the answers are incredibly important in understanding research participants' lives. In the span of most in-depth interviews, the discussion of commuting might last only a minute or two, but by experiencing a city's commute for yourself you gain a better sense of the mental and physical state in which people arrive for work or school in the morning and back home in the evening.

If you're trying to understand people's motivations, think

about the different frames of mind they could be in if they'd just spent thirty minutes in gridlock on the 405 in Los Angeles compared with a packed but highly efficient subway ride in Tokyo or Singapore. These are fundamentally different experiences that affect everything from scheduling business meetings to making phone calls or sending messages. China is already the world's largest car market and is growing at a fair pace, and snail's-pace traffic is already the norm.

How would a Chinese in-car experience be designed differently when the driver has significantly more time to interact with the display? Or when the hassle of driving and parking reaches the point that it makes more sense to hire a dedicated driver with a very different level of education to the owner? Or when the local shy-distance between vehicles (the mentally comfortable space that we prefer to have when negotiating the road with other vehicles) is measured in single-digit inches? The opportunities flow out of the observations and firsthand experiences.

Long-Distance Travel, sans the Travel

Airports, train stations, and intercity bus stations are renowned among people-watchers (of both the professional and dilettante varieties) for the diverse crowds that pass through their halls. Beyond the broad range of fashion sensibilities and group dynamics you might find in these places, you'll also find a host of opportunities to calibrate to the local culture.

Stations for medium- to long-distance travel exist in every city and support a similar range of activities, which make them ripe for cross-cultural comparisons. Some particularly revealing behaviors (in terms of cultural variance) to look for include queuing behaviors, payment options at shops and kiosks, the sale and consumption of entertainment media for the trip, snack and beverage preferences, and the use of personal technologies in waiting areas.

Even the simplest piece of infrastructure, the waiting area, can speak volumes about the local culture. In India there will be one waiting room for men and women, and another for women and children only; in the United Kingdom you'll find one waiting room for all comers; in Japan it's mostly the same, but with the likelihood of a separate smoking room nearby; and in China, where one might expect egalitarianism to rule, you will likely see three separate waiting rooms—one that's open for all, another for military personnel, and a third for VIPs who are willing to pay a small fee for access or whose credit card or bank provide the service as a value-added offering.

Travel hubs, as potential targets for high-profile terror attacks, also tend to reveal norms and expectations about security (or security theater) and the level of government suspicion toward its populace, from the presence of armed guards and sniffer dogs to the use of ID cards, restrictions on passenger movement, and whether bags are scanned on entry (as today they are at many long-distance Chinese train stations). As sensitive spaces, travel hubs are also good places for researchers (or voyeurs) to practice rapidly and discreetly capturing photos and video, and in some cases to practice negotiating with security authorities once detained. Places to leave things (for example, lockers, waste bins, and lost-and-founds) are likely absent in a country learning to live with a sustained bombing campaign. As you might expect for a city in a country that has been at war since the turn of the century, it's no surprise that New York remains one of the more paranoid places on the planet, only trumped by the recently seceded Juba in South Sudan.* Even if locals the world over don't agree with the reasons behind the security, they very quickly become used to its norms, making it harder (for them) to spot opportunities or outliers.

Some airports are more interesting than others. The now-defunct Dubai Terminal 2 served a range of destinations including Kabul, Kish, Kandahar, Baghdad, and Mogadishu, with burly contractors, NGO staff, wealthy local businessmen, and con artists milling around check-in gates to lively destinations—the kind of place where you smile when a flight is delayed and you're handed an opportunity to watch and learn.

The Hairdresser, the Barbershop

Every community has some form of social hub where people come together, hang out, and catch up on gossip—effectively a stock market trading on social currency. In many communities, that hub is the hairdresser or barbershop. It would be difficult to design a space more conducive to engaging in social interaction: somewhere to sit and wait; neither too quiet nor too noisy; lots of mirrors for scanning the room and catching facial expressions; a task that can take twenty minutes to an hour to com-

---

* I prefer to conduct research in the latter, if for no other reason than that the paranoia is easier to justify.

plete; and where the focus is on the interaction between the barber or hairdresser and the client, rather than the usual distractions of mobile phones or otherwise. For the price of a cut or shave, that seat is as much yours as any local's, and once you're in it you have as much right to steer the conversation as anyone in the room. Gender aside, almost anyone can walk through the doors and be served. I usually try to hit a different barber every day for a shave, and on a few occasions I've gone to two in the same day.*

Through these conversations, you can figure out the best places to go to and explore attitudes on pretty much any topic under the sun, from sports teams to the appropriate local moves for men and women to pick someone up, to the level of corruption in government. It's also a good way to find leads on people to interview who know the most about how the community has changed and can connect you to other social connectors. Think of it as hyperlocal search with directions and personal connections built in. Pay for a fresh blade, figure out where you want the conversation to go, and enjoy the ride.

---

* And along the way I've experienced some of the more bloody, painful, and downright exotic variations of a straight-up shave: blunt razors the world over; chunks of face taken off me by branded-but-fake Gillette razors in Lhasa; the joys of thread hair-plucking in Istanbul; raw aloe rubbed onto scarred wounds in Bangalore; shaves in shops, on the street, and even in a field; electric shaves in a Ghanaian community with frequent power cuts (in a community with a high HIV rate, locals considered the electric option less likely to transmit the virus than blades); through to value-added services such as having my ears cleaned out by razor blades in Hue, Vietnam.

Breaching Behaviors

There was a time when it was unacceptable for a gentleman to go out in public without wearing a hat. And there was a time when the idea of walking around town and blocking out the sounds of the city with headphones and music was considered outlandish. The notion of sharing the minutiae of everyday life with complete strangers would have been considered a sign of a demented mind. But perceptions, and social norms, change. It's not always directly evident what norms are in play, as they can vary between social classes, groups, times, and places and can even appear to be contradictory. Taking a drink in one context can be as antisocial as declining the offer of a drink in another.

A firsthand exploration of the line between "acceptable" and "unacceptable" can be both nerve-racking and intellectually rewarding. It's also a great tool for uncovering issues that might negatively affect adoption of a particular product or service, and to test the malleability of the social norms in question. The greater the affront caused by a small act of impoliteness, the harder and faster the unwritten rule.

The most famous breaching experiment was conducted in 1974 by Stanley Milgram and his Yale students, who tested the unwritten "first-come, first-served" seating rule on New York subways by approaching passengers and asking them for their seats. Surprisingly, 68 percent of passengers obliged. Ironically, the experiment seemed to cause more pain for the experimenters tasked with crossing the social boundary than for the people who gave up their seats. "I was afraid I was going to throw up," said one of the students recalling the experience. Milgram, in an interview with *Psychology Today*, described the deep anxiety and discomfort he went through upon his first crack at the experiment: "The words seemed lodged in my trachea and would simply not emerge." After scolding himself and mustering the strength to ask for a seat, his anxiety turned to shame. "Taking the man's seat, I was overwhelmed by the need to behave in a way that would justify my request," he said. "My head sank between my knees, and I could feel my face blanching. I was not role-playing. I actually felt as if I were going to perish."

Breaching doesn't always have to be an act of emotional masochism, and in certain high-risk situations (especially where armed guards are involved) it may not be worthwhile to put your safety on the line. But there is much empathic understanding to be gained from breaching, and there are many ways to test the impact of crossing a line, from role-play within the team to staged situations out in the field to small impromptu interventions when you sense the possibility of an enlightening experience. Breaching activities can include: jumping a line; talking loudly on a mobile phone in close quarters with strangers, such as in an elevator or train; placing a pile of cash on a dining table during a meal; or wearing a nonworking prototype of a potential new product like video-player sunglasses and acting out the user experience in public (all of which I and/or my team members have done on recent research studies).

The International Language of "Lovin' It"

It might seem contradictory to the sentiment of this book to travel halfway around the world to visit a McDonald's, but the value of the experience has little to do with the flavor of the food and much to do with the tastes of the local clientele.

Of all our activities, eating is probably the most deeply engrained in our psyche, culturally grounded in an incredibly diverse set of assumptions we learn from childhood: from what we consider "normal" food to how we're supposed to prepare it, purchase it, eat it, and share it. Regardless of your opinion on the menus and business practices at multinational restaurant chains, the very nature of the industry and its commercial sustainability is predicated on figuring out how to appeal to the nuanced mass sensibilities in every market, across a huge spectrum of cultures.

International chains are therefore valuable reference points for calibration: heavily frequented by younger locals (and in many instances considered regional rather than international enterprises), with tailored offerings and branding elements interspersed among the global hallmarks. The fact that you can find a McDonald's in more than thirty thousand locations in the world means you can compare everything in one country's McDonald's—the customers, the food, the menus, the decor, and the behaviors within and around it—with any other's. By thinking through its design decisions, you can see how a multinational brand has tailored its offerings to a particular setting and culture.

While many chains, particularly fast food, may be considered down-market establishments in developed countries, they're often considered aspirational in developing markets, with luxury amenities like guaranteed air-conditioning and consistently well-maintained restrooms.

Take a McDonald's in Mumbai: the easiest difference to spot compared with one in, say, Paris is in the menu—half of which is vegetarian. The McAloo Tikki, a potato-, peas-, and bread-based patty between two buns, reigns supreme sales-wise, alongside local equivalents of signature items, such as the (big, but not Big) Maharaja-Mac, a double layer of chicken breast with gooey cheese, lettuce, and tomato sandwiched between its buns. Unsurprisingly, for a country with a high percentage of Hindus (for whom cows are sacred) and Muslims (who don't eat pork), the packaging clearly indicates vegetarian food, with a green dot in a green square, and nonvegetarian food, with a brown dot in a brown square.* The restaurant also contains two completely separated kitchens, one for preparing meat and the other for vegetarian foods, with utensils and staff kept separate as well.

As a high-volume fast-food joint, McDonald's tends to invest early in infrastructure that can shave seconds off a transaction time, so you're likely to see what payment options the masses there have most recently adopted. Out in the restaurant, you can observe group dynamics and ranges of distribution, as well as imagery depicting the corporate interpretations of local youth aspirations; in one particular McDonald's in China, I noticed an image with smiling, socially engaged teens on laptops, accompanied by the word *modern* spelled out in English.

In a more developed market such as Japan, twenty-four-hour McDonald's restaurants are often the overnight accommodation

---

* Meat and nonmeat markings are locally mandated by law, with the possible exception of a fully vegetarian restaurant near a high-traffic Hindu shrine.

of choice for homeless people and those waiting for the public transport to start. For the price of a cup of coffee, they can rest their heads on tabletops undisturbed.

Reading the Signs

Ubiquitous as it may be, signage is often ignored by passersby, with the exception of certain life-and-death situations. But for the avid observer wanting to get a read on the urban environment, signs, and the underlying motivations that brought them into being, can say a great deal about social behavior and value conflicts in public spaces.

Urban signs come in many flavors: directions, street signs, a handwritten note regarding a lost pet, another note announcing a found set of keys. But the ones that can be most revealing about current and changing societal assumptions are of the "do this" and "don't do that" variety.

Official do-don't signs put up by the local authorities often reflect a stress point between existing behaviors and the preferences of the greater community, or at least the decision-makers who mandate the signage. "Don't litter" signs are a clear response to the persistent issue of littering and can be found all over the world. The "no fireworks" signs in China are a response to the long-standing practice of igniting fireworks to celebrate a birth, death, business opening, or holiday, a tradition that has come under scrutiny because of the risk of fire, quite famously after the blaze that engulfed part of the China Central Television (CCTV) complex in Beijing during the 2009 Chinese New Year celebration. The crackdown also reflects a shift from low-rise housing, where the noise might affect only the residents of a dozen or so homes, to high-rise apartment blocks with acoustic properties that ensure the noise from a single celebration will be heard by hundreds of families.

The mere existence of a sign reveals that whatever issue it pertains to is important enough for someone, presumably an authority on the matter, to invest time and energy to discuss the possibility of a formal or informal ban with other people in the know, commission production of the sign (or urge someone else to rubber-stamp it), and have it installed. That someone has either the legal or moral right to put up a sign in a given location reveals standards and assumptions about who is allowed to do so.

In most instances, these signs aren't put in place to issue firm directives and control behavior (much as authoritarian urban planners might fantasize); they're there because the person(s) who wants to control behavior lacks the power or presence to do so and believes an authoritative-seeming sign can serve as enforcer. Many formal do-don't signs come with a "by the authority of" tagline: "By the authority of the Surgeon General" or "By the authority of Mayor So-and-So." Such signs are often the one piece of urban infrastructure that retains the mayor's name after all his other prestige developments have fallen by the wayside. But most of the time we don't pay any attention to the do-don't signs; if we ever did, we've long since absorbed the information and developed the habit of ignoring them.

Some signs are displayed to limit legal liability. "Don't lean on the rail" comes with a set of assumptions that if you do end up falling off the building and breaking a leg, the building owner's legal liability will be limited, or at least that case will be made in court. The same goes for signs like "infants must be carried," found on escalators, and "keep your feet away from the edges."

In countries that are officially multilingual, such as Canada, the languages that need to appear on official signs are enshrined in the constitution. The order in which the languages appear on a sign can be associated with one given prominence over the other(s), and in some communities this becomes a highly politicized issue. In India, Hindi is the official state language, but English enjoys the status of subsidiary official language, and there are fourteen other official languages: Assamese, Bengali, Gujarati, Kannada, Kashmiri, Malayalam, Marathi, Oriya, Punjabi, Sanskrit, Sindhi, Tamil, Telugu, and Urdu. The spread of signage supporting a particular language can reflect migratory flows, shifts in vacationing preferences, a willingness to accept foreigners in an erstwhile closed society, and an increasing importance of trade between nations. Chinese signs have become increasingly prevalent in Africa at the beginning of the twenty-first century. English has been widely adopted on the Beijing Metro. The layout of bilingual signs in Arabic equally support two sets of cultural assumptions: Arabic text running from right to left and Western scripts from left to right.

The language used on a sign can also reveal the aspirations of its authors. In Japan, some shops display signs that are only in English—not for the benefit of English-speaking customers, but in order to lend a cosmopolitan air to the establishment. A similar rationale is inherent in the design of T-shirts and other paraphernalia displaying Japanese text worn by Westerners with no knowledge of that language. The inappropriate use of Japanese kanji for tattoos has, and will continue to, provide mirth to those who actually understand their meaning. As the world starts to appreciate the nuances of Chinese culture, expect more of the products and services created by Chinese designers to be laden with their cultural hallmarks.

In cultures with high levels of illiteracy, it's far more acceptable for an illiterate person to rely on human directions rather than signs. For instance, an illiterate auto-rickshaw driver in New Delhi traveling a route well outside his comfort zone is either going to stop the vehicle and ask for directions or phone a friend. One of the most comprehensive examples of urban signage supporting illiterate use can be found in the iconography designed by Lance Wyman for the Mexico City Metro in 1968, at a time when Mexico still had a significant level of illiteracy—with each station having a simple icon such as a duck, cannon, or bell, corresponding to a nearby cultural or historical landmark.

Some signs document the evolution of technology. The phone depicted in "no mobile phones" sign has evolved over the years from Motorola's iconic brick to Nokia's Candybar to Apple's iPhone, with each generation in turn looking as outdated as the next, at least until the form factor settles or usage disappears. You can still see the old-school rotary dial phone in pictograms for telephonic services in Egypt.

Occasionally there's a subtle subversiveness to be found in formal signs, where the attention to detail in the "don't" element of the sign conflicts with a nuanced understanding of the demand being made. In Tokyo I came across a "no cycling" sign that took the classic posture of a fixed-gear enthusiast, whose silhouetted bike revealed keirin geometry, bullhorn bars, and no brakes—little details that a trained eye would notice, and which were clearly used intentionally by an in-the-know designer as a subversive wink and nod to fellow cyclists.

"Don't" signs can also produce subcultural and countercultural gems. "Don't practice your golf swing" seen in a petite neighborhood park in Tokyo says as much about the sporting preferences of middle-aged Japanese men and women as it does about the dangers of that activity in that space. The presence of the sign suggests that there is actually some possibility of the prohibited activity taking place there. Why doesn't that park have a "don't practice your baseball swing" sign, given that baseball is the de facto national sport in Japan and could be as much of a hazard to park-goers? For starters, baseball activity tends to be confined to designated baseball facilities. Tokyo has many small neighborhood golf ranges, but they charge an entry fee, whereas the park is free. The sign itself provides none of this information, of course, but it goes to show that the presence of certain signs, and the absence of others, can tell you a great deal about how a public space is used and how its constituents think it ought to be used.

In countries with a dense population, where one person's discourteous act can impact many others in close proximity, the rules governing courtesy behaviors are often articulated in excruciating detail. The Tokyo subway's signs specify a range of activities that occur with sufficient frequency to require public censure: no smoking, no groping, no speaking on a mobile phone, no music, no applying makeup, no jumping on the train as the doors are closing, no sleeping on the floor, no food or drink, and so on.

A lack of signage can be just as revealing. On one field study in Iran, our team took a late-night stroll in northern Tehran and wandered around a park. There were only two signs in the whole park: "drink this water" and, at another source, "don't drink this water." A comparable park in the United States, arguably one of the more officious countries in the world, is likely to be filled with signs detailing rules and regulations, do's and don'ts, and especially so in children's play areas. Still, whether a park is in Iran, America, or any other part of the world, this form of signage can be an indicator of the regulatory environment in the city, state, or country.

Which is more sophisticated? A country that articulates its rules and regulations through the use of physical, in-your-face signs, or one where the assumptions about what you can and can't do are more inherent in the social fabric of society? Does a lack of signage reveal a lack of process, thought, conclusion, rule of law? Or the opposite?

In many ways a sign can be a last resort, a footnote to a space whose purpose could and perhaps should have been planned better for intuitive use, sans written directions. Urban planners, architects, and designers have created a whole vocabulary of uncomfortable addendums—urban forms with cues to influence behaviors—such as rows of small spikes to stop people from sitting on ledges or low flat walls; metal bobbles welded to rails to keep skateboarders off; and starbursts of spikes on pigeon-prone surfaces.

As you train your eyes on a city's signage, be sure to consider how it might evolve in a more digitized future. If we become increasingly able to create digital layers and overlay them on the world around us, then in theory anyone who could create a layer would be able to post signs or commentary, and anyone who knows how to find those layers would be able to view them. And if the people putting up signs, from government agencies to advertisers, are able to use more and more sophisticated cameras and sensors to take stock of passersby, how will they use that data to convey authority? "No smoking" signs might carry a much more authoritative ring if they were accompanied by the image and voice of your strict-disciplinarian high school math teacher.

Capturing the Platzgeist

Designers often talk of staying in step with the zeitgeist, a German term that translates literally as "time spirit" but is in itself far from a literal substance. The zeitgeist is much bigger than contemporary trends and styles: it's a mood, an essence, and through cultural absorption a good designer can gain an intuition about whether designs are congruous or incongruous with the zeitgeist.

The same can be said about what I like to call the platzgeist, a gestalt sense of the spirit of an environment, whether a neighborhood, city, region, or country. All of the above techniques can help you gain that sense, both consciously and subconsciously, but by capturing it through sensory stimuli, you can create a veritable mood database. And after your sense of platzgeist has faded over time, this database will be your return ticket to that place and its spirit.

Macro tours, capturing imagery around an environment through a macro (extreme close-up) camera lens, allow you to think about the little things, literally: the textures, colors, geometry, and patina that make up an object or space, capturing and experiencing things up close. A macro lens allows you to isolate things from their context, but the images you capture can later be viewed in clusters to give a sense of cumulative effect.

A macro tour can be done as a walking tour around a neighborhood or confined within a more limited space, such as a convenience store, bus interior, or public park. The macro tour works best when conducted by multiple teams, so that in follow-up meetings the photos from different team members can be aggregated, arranged, pinned up, and shared. The detail and depth of field inherent in macro photography also make great material for presentations, experience boards, and movies later on.

Some variations on the macro tour include the fish-eye tour (using an extreme wide-angle lens instead of a close-up one) and the panorama tour, capturing as much of an environment as possible within single images. In contrast to the high-resolution, blinders-on detail of the macro tour, the fisheye and panorama tours foster a big-picture hyperawareness of a setting, and this counterpoint of zoomed-in and zoomed-out provides an arrayed perspective ideal for absorbing the platzgeist.

Since the goal of these activities is to capture the sensory experience within a setting, it helps to go beyond visual stimuli. Of course, it can be tough to record and play back smells, tastes, and tactile experiences (though it will be possible someday), but an audio tour can add a wonderful layer of texture to the process.

"Silence" is rarely truly silent—it's just that we've trained our ears to filter out the ambient noise. A high-end audio recorder allows you to reimagine an environment by picking up the sounds that otherwise drift by: a single pair of high-heeled shoes among a herd of commuting flat-soles, a crying child off in the distance, the pings and dings of machines' audio interfaces. Back at the office, audio tour recordings can be played during synthesis sessions and workshops to re-create the environment where the data was collected and jog the team's sensory memories, and can also be overlaid as audio tracks to add depth to concept movies.

When the World Is at Your Doorstep, Don't Just Look out the Window

The cultural calibration techniques outlined in this chapter are designed to be as enjoyable as they are inspirational, but when it comes to corporate research there's always that lingering question: are they practical? Even when they don't cut into the formal research schedule, they still carry a cost in terms of time and energy, usually bore by the team in the form of long days if not sleep deprivation.*

Let's take it in practical terms, then. Perhaps you're trying to design, for instance, a microwave oven optimized for a particular demographic. How does a more nuanced understanding of locals' commuting habits help you accomplish such a task? If those locals are your consumers, then by understanding their

---

* A good rule of thumb for any research team leaders: if you plan to implement any of these techniques, be sure to do so in a way that is, at the very least, as rewarding to your team as a bonus hour of sleep after a week straight of four-hour nights.

commute you might gain some distinct insight on the pressures that lead them to zap their food and eat it on the go; you might even get a glimpse of how they eat on public transit, openly or furtively depending on what the formal and informal rules of the environment allow.

In a broader sense, though, it can help you understand how your consumers live and how they aspire to live, the daily challenges they face, and how they find a balance between convenience, cost, and comfort. When you interview consumers directly and visit their homes, the commute and any of these other contextual activities will only serve to augment your understanding of the things they share with you, in a way that assumptions based on demographic characteristics simply can't.

The trick to these cultural calibration techniques is striking the right balance, so they don't feel like overstimulation. Proper implementation involves constantly taking the pulse of how much you and your team have absorbed and how much energy you've expended in the process. There's no such thing as too much learning (although novice teams often overcollect data), but there is always a point of diminishing returns, and the smart (and often brave) choice is to step away and focus on methods that will yield richer results.

Often what separates good design research from great design research is finding the right balance between formal and informal data collection, and having the right mental and physical space to process it—in essence moving data (raw information) into insight (cogently applying the data to the task at hand). Most researchers learn the formal methods but struggle with their conscience (and their clients') to justify activities that feel less like work and more like having fun. I call this "finding the optimal *surface area*" and it's one of eight principles of design research I've listed in an appendix in the back of this book.

Our ability to imagine what-could-be stems from knowledge, amplified by experiences, and ultimately our ability to understand which of those experiences can be applied to the task at hand. Whether you're starting a new business, designing something discrete, or trying to figure out your next career move, rapid calibration techniques and the ability to spot what's hidden in plain sight will help you find your way there. Bringing that back into your life and work will help you challenge minds and move hearts. Figure this out and wallets will open themselves.

Chapter 6

A Matter of Trust

On July 8, 1849, the *New York Herald* reported that one William Thompson, "a man of genteel appearance," had developed a reputation for casually approaching strangers on the streets of New York and striking up a conversation. After winning them over with banter, he would very literally put their faith to a test, asking, "Have you confidence in me to trust me with your watch until to-morrow[?]" Those who replied in the affirmative would hand over their watches, and Thompson would walk away laughing. So would the victims, who presupposed that a man so friendly, and with such a brazen proposition, would surely have been worthy of their trust. Of course, none of them saw Thompson—or their watches—again, until a Thomas McDonald, who had "loaned" Thompson a $110 gold watch (roughly $3,000 in 2012 dollars) two months prior, spotted him on the street and promptly flagged down a police officer to make an arrest.

When word of this strange crime spread, Thompson came to be known as the "Confidence Man." The story became the inspiration for Herman Melville's last novel, *The Confidence-Man: His Masquerade*, and gave rise to the term we still use today to describe those experts at winning, manipulating, and exploiting the trust of strangers: con men.

William Thompson may have been the original con man, but the tale of the perils of misplaced trust goes all the way back to Genesis, when the serpent, "more subtle than any beast of the field," deceived Adam and Eve in the Garden of Eden. This most foundational of lessons in human history speaks to the role of trust as the most fundamental force shaping every form of human interaction.

Trust is indispensable to everything we do: every social connection and every business transaction; every vote and every treaty; every yes and every no. We can't live without trust, and we can't survive without some degree of mistrust. Our sense of what is sufficiently trustworthy or untrustworthy is part of our personal and cultural identity, finely honed to the point that we deride those who trust too much as naive and those who trust too little as paranoid.

Who would even consider handing a $3,000 watch over to a complete stranger on the streets of Manhattan these days (or heeding the suggestions of a talking snake, for that matter)? And who bothers to read all the way through any email that begins "I am the son of a Nigerian prince and I need your assistance"? Our standards may change over time, but they do so in ways that we can often anticipate, on scales both large and small. And with that we'll take a journey across the globe to explore why we trust some things, people, and brands more than others and what it takes to build and maintain trust, starting with a trip to the Middle Kingdom.

It's midmorning, midwinter and you're taking a brisk walk through a traditional gray-walled Beijing neighborhood, looking to keep the intense cold at bay and find somewhere with a bit of warmth and a bite to eat. Tomorrow you fly to Tokyo for a client pitch meeting and want to be on top of your game. A chimney stack of steaming bamboo baskets filled with dumplings, tended by a squat lady with a weathered face and a smeared apron, beckons. Do you trust that a plate of dumplings from this stall is safe to eat? What are the consequences of being wrong? What are the cues that provide supporting evidence either way? Do you trust your assessment of those cues?

One week and six thousand air miles later you're standing in a Starbucks in San Francisco, pausing momentarily in front of the condiments counter before pouring liquid into your cup from a finger-stained thermos with a peeling, blurry label marked "half-and-half." How many people have touched this thermos? How many of those went to the bathroom and didn't wash their hands? Is it safe to consume? Again, what are the cues that provide supporting evidence either way? What are the consequences if it isn't?

At the very moment you make a decision, whether you're standing in front of a neighborhood dumpling stall or at the half-and-half thermos in a major restaurant chain, you're implicitly and explicitly considering things both large and small: from contextual clues like whether other customers are present and taking on the risk themselves, to a lifetime's worth of experiences in these kinds of contexts; the value of the brand and what it stands for; to the impact if things go wrong. All the scenarios and all the clues come to bear on this single moment.

Much like a biological ecosystem, the *trust ecosystem*—the context in which we make each trust-distrust decision, characterized by the surrounding environment and all its players, from the local (or hyperlocal) crime rate to the sights and smells at hand to the friendliness of strangers—shapes each and every interaction that takes place within it. And like a biological ecosystem, when broad systemic changes take place in a trust ecosystem, everything and everyone within it feels the effects.

Breaking Down the Gestalt of Trust

Before we start examining trust by exploring its ecosystem, let's take a look at how we actually evaluate the trustworthiness of products and services. There is no simple formula, and trust decisions can be based on anything from a vague sentiment—something seems shady, hinky, or amiss, or it just feels right—to a heuristic, or simple psychological shortcut. For instance, we might refuse to eat anywhere that doesn't have at least four stars on a trusted restaurant reviews site, but would be willing to make an exception when a foodie friend makes an implicit recommendation by "checking in" (via a social network like Foursquare) somewhere unexpected. Indeed, this heuristic is the basis for the threshold model of adoption discussed in chapter 3, which illustrates how social networks, trust ecosystems in and of themselves, hold tremendous sway over decision-making processes.

As you might expect from something so fantastically complex, there are many different ways to approach trust, a quality so definitive of our decision-making and yet so reliant on intuiting massive amounts of information, where one tiny detail could be the difference between fear and comfort. But between the sum (an entire trust ecosystem) and all its parts (each clue), trust has its basis in certain elements of survival, and the preservation of our basic resources for survival. For the sake of structure, let's take six general dimensions on which we evaluate trustworthiness: authenticity, fulfillment, value, reliability, safety, and recourse.

When a product possesses qualities consistent with our expectations of what that product should contain, we consider it authentic, even if that authenticity is subjective and culturally dependent. Take pizza: an authentic pizza to a New Yorker has a thin, chewy crust and a light sauce, whereas an authentic pizza to a Chicagoan has a thick crust and chunky sauce. However, if a restaurateur in either city tried to serve a pizza made with a buttery pastry, ketchup, and processed cheese, customers would rapidly lose faith in the business and its ability to produce something that fit their definition of "pizza."

Fulfillment, in the immortal words of the British wood stain and preservative brand Ronseal, is when a product "does exactly what it says on the tin." We trust those things that live up to their claims and distrust those that fall short.

Value can be defined as a level of quality commensurate with price relative to alternatives; in simpler terms, we trust things that don't feel like a rip-off.

Reliability is similar to fulfillment, but it also means a product does what it's supposed to with enough consistency that we can count on it performing in those moments when we need it the most. It will still be around tomorrow, and the day after tomorrow, and the day after that.

Safety is an easy one: we don't trust things that we believe will cause serious physical or psychological damage to ourselves, others, or the environment.

Finally, recourse is a sense of assurance, either explicit or implicit, that if a product fails or breaks down, the manufacturer or retailer will deal with the problem in a timely and courteous manner. Explicit recourse could be a warranty, a customer service lifeline, a replacement policy, or a money-back guarantee.

What do these six facets of trust have in common? They can all be standardized, codified, and enforced through consumer protection legislation like truth-in-advertising laws, lemon laws, and health and safety codes, but the laws and levels of enforcement can vary widely from one context to another, just as individuals' subjective assessments of all six will vary depending on the past experiences and available information they have at their disposal. Between that regulatory protection and those subjective assessments, a set of expectations is created that defines the trust ecosystem.

In a high-trust consumer ecosystem, customers expect merchants to offer reliable goods and services at reasonable prices, they expect a high degree of truth in marketing, and they expect the government (or juries of their peers) to have their backs in the event of gross violations of trust. In turn, the merchants in a high-trust ecosystem expect customers to take their offerings and their marketing pitches at face value. Conversely, in a low-trust consumer ecosystem, customers are far more likely to be dubious of most offerings and lack the peace of mind of a regulatory safety net. Merchants must assume that the burden of proof is on them, but they also know that they can get away with more because they don't face the threat of fines or litigation. Obviously consumers in high- and low-trust ecosystems operate under very different default assumptions, respectively: either that things are trustworthy until red flags are raised, or that things are untrustworthy until fears are allayed.

We can think of these default assumptions as different starting points on a threshold map of trust, where the area below the trough threshold is the zone of rejection, the area above the peak threshold is the zone of complete faith, and the area in between is the zone of sufficient trust. In the zone of rejection, the consumer refuses to use the product or service in question because she expects its benefit to fall short of its cost (in terms of money, health, prestige, or whatever criteria she deems important at purchase). In the zone of sufficient trust, there is at least some willingness to consume, but there is also some degree of skepticism that keeps the consumer on alert for any potential deal-breakers. In the zone of complete faith, the consumer has 100 percent confidence that the product or service will deliver on every promise, which means there's no need to waste any energy looking for flaws or planning for contingencies.

Let's go back to those two scenarios I put forth earlier: the dumpling stall in Beijing and the half-and-half thermos in San Francisco. By most global metrics, China is a low-consumer-trust ecosystem, particularly when it comes to food. Over the course of any given year, news stories emerge about tainted foods, from false eggs made from chemicals, gelatin, and paraffin to duck meat marinated in sheep urine in order to give it the smell and taste of lamb to so-called gutter oil, saturated oils reclaimed from industrial kitchens and, occasionally, an actual gutter. The starting point on the threshold map of trust is likely to lie squarely in the zone of rejection. How does a restaurateur move a potential customer into the zone of sufficient trust? He could change the decor, redesign the menu, hang up some press clippings with rave reviews, maybe even raise prices to make the place seem a little fancier—or he could make a more direct connection between the starting product and what ends up on your plate. When the plate of chicken arrives, you know it's chicken because the body, feet, wings, and head are laid out on the plate, reinforcing its origins. (Start with the head and work down—chicken feet are a delicacy in China.) In low-trust ecosystems the level of abstraction between the animal that was slaughtered and the food that appears on your plate is generally lower than in higher-trust ecosystems.

Now let's head back to that Starbucks in San Francisco. Not only are we in a country, state, and city with relatively high (and adequately enforced) consumer protection standards, but we're in an establishment with corporate safety standards as well. The default assumption in this environment is that a half-and-half thermos is perfectly safe, as long as everything in this particular Starbucks appears consistent with those standards. However, any indicator that safety has been compromised—spills that have been left uncleaned by inattentive staff, flies circling around the half-and-half—might make you think twice about consuming it. As for the coffee you'd be pouring it into, you could mull over its authenticity (is it really fair-trade?), fulfillment (will they serve you decaf if you ask for decaf?), value (are you getting your $3 worth?), reliability (will it taste as good as that cup you had yesterday?), safety (will the cup lid stay in place as you walk to the car, or will the contents spill and scald you?), and recourse (can you get a fresh cup or your money back if it happens to taste like charred dirt?). But because Starbucks is generally considered a trusted brand in terms of these metrics, the name on the door becomes the heuristic that allows you to save mental energy and take the leap of faith.

The Power of Brands

Brands play a prominent role in the trust ecosystem: every time we encounter a new product under the umbrella of a known brand, our baseline level of trust in that product is shaped by the experiences we've had with other products from that brand. Levels of trust in brands have been shown to correlate strongly with loyalty to brands and positive emotional associations with them, both of which contribute to brands' market share and a company's ability to charge a premium.

Trust in a brand also influences people's willingness to believe statements they hear about that brand. According to the consulting firm Edelman's Trust Barometer index, when a company is trusted, 51 percent of people are willing to believe positive information about the company after hearing it once or twice, while only 25 percent will believe negative information the first couple of times they hear it. But when a company is distrusted, 57 percent will believe negative information about the company after hearing it once or twice, and a mere 15 percent will believe positive information. Trust can be a major asset for a brand, but a lack of it can be devastating even more.

If we think about branding in terms of these six dimensions— authenticity, fulfillment, value, reliability, safety, and recourse— we can identify major benefits of establishing a known brand name. The consistency that makes a Coke a Coke suggests: authenticity, because a Coke always tastes the way you know and expect it to taste; fulfillment, because you know the effect it had on you before and you expect it to have the same effect again; value, because when you've paid, say, a dollar for a bottle of Coke in the past, it creates a lasting impression that your next bottle of Coke will be worth a dollar to you, thanks to the cognitive bias known as the anchoring effect; reliability, because, again, Coke tastes about the same every time; and safety, because if it hasn't hurt you before you can reasonably expect it not to hurt you the next time you drink it (notwithstanding long-term health problems now blamed on sugary drinks). If a brand can maintain that consistency, there's little need for recourse, theoretically, because that set of assumptions would instill complete faith* and put the thought of recourse out of the consumer's mind.

Given the trust that consumers put into certain brands, it's no surprise that competitors are willing to copy, steal, or other-

---

* Coke also provides the cautionary tale of what can go wrong when a brand messes with its core product and values, as we learned from the 1985 failure of New Coke, where a reformulated recipe caused a huge uproar and exacted a cost on the company trust ecosystem. Fortunately, Coke's executives responded to customer outrage and put the original recipe back on the market in a span of seventy-nine days, thus salvaging their reputation.

wise pay homage to existing brands in order to sell more of their own product. We're all familiar with near-replica products such as sunglasses and mobile phones that appear remarkably similar to other products on the market, and although brands, consumers, and legal authorities might at times disagree on what constitutes "fake," we've all seen brand names appear in some, ahem, questionable places.

The most radical example I've come across was in the Kabul branch of KFC—at least it looked and smelled like a KFC, with Colonel Sanders's familiar face and the iconic red and white KFC color scheme, accompanied by the unmistakable smell of fried batter. But the parent company, Yum! Brands, didn't have any franchisees in the country. A local entrepreneur had replicated the brand's signage and set up his own outlet, in this instance called Kabul Fried Chicken. That someone in a war-torn country can reverse-engineer an entire fast-food joint is remarkable enough, but it was where he decided to break with simply copying what exists in other countries and adapt the design to local conventions that piqued my interest.

If you enter a real KFC (or pretty much any international fast-food chain, for that matter), the one thing you won't see represented on menus or signage is the original animal that the food has come from. In the world of higher-trust ecosystems, fast-food companies put as much distance as possible between the origins of meat and the product that appears on the plate. Not so in Kabul, where the one addition to the signage was a photorealistic picture of a chicken (the addition of kebabs to the menu may also have been a giveaway that this was not a real KFC, though as we saw in chapter 5 with the McAloo, fast-food companies are often willing to adapt menus to local tastes). In a country where "chicken" may not actually be chicken, the consumer needs reassurance.

In the context of this particular trust ecosystem, authenticity depends most on establishing a direct connection between the food products served—in this case, chicken—and their origins. Trust is engendered by showing that the food served is authentic, not by establishing that the restaurant itself is an official KFC-authorized franchise.

If a KFC (a "real" one) in Kentucky were to use the live chicken imagery and serve kebabs as Kabul Fried Chicken does, its customers might lose trust in the brand because these new additions would be strikingly inconsistent with what KFC fans have come to expect from the brand. As Coke's leaders found when they misguidedly introduced New Coke, consumers will decide what's authentic and what's not. Just ask the makers of Life Savers soda, Colgate kitchen entrees, Ben-Gay aspirin, Bic underwear, or Smith & Wesson mountain bikes—all real offerings that flopped, despite their pedigrees.

Sniffing the Milk

When I was fresh out of college in the mid-'90s, I taught a design course at the University of London's Birkbeck College. One of the assignments I gave some web design students prompted them to think about the nuances of designing a process such as e-commerce by having them deconstruct, step by step, the familiar task of making a cup of tea. Most of the students identified a simple flow to the tea-making process: walk into the kitchen, fill the kettle with water, turn on the stove, put the kettle on the stove, select a particular kind of tea from among several options . . . you get the picture. There was some variation in the class over whether to put tea into the pot before turning on the kettle; which type of tea to use (the same question in China or India would likely yield a very different answer); whether they had an electric kettle or used a gas stove; and whether they took sugar or not. But when I asked if anyone incorporated some other step that none of the others mentioned, only one student raised his hand and said something that was both outside most people's normal parameters and yet entirely rational: "Sniff the milk." He was a bachelor who lived alone, spent little time in his flat, and hardly kept to a regular grocery-shopping schedule. As a result, he often found that his milk would spoil before he used it all up; sniffing it was his method of determining whether he could trust that it was safe to consume.

Thinking back to our Starbucks example, what's the difference between sniffing the milk in a global brand's shop and sniffing it at home? At Starbucks, dozens of indicators signal to consumers that the milk is trustworthy, from the health inspector's grade on the door to the condensation on the outside of the thermos indicating it has recently come out of the fridge to the appearance of busy staff regularly replacing thermoses that have been sitting out with new ones. At home, the only indicator is the expiration date stamped on the carton, which may provide some confidence in the product but doesn't actually tell you when it will definitively sour. We all have sniff tests in our lives—

things we do to reassure us at critical stages of consumption or interaction that a product or service (or person) is worthy of our trust. Knowing the trust ecosystem in which consumers operate and knowing which positive cues will reinforce trust or allay concern is a matter that all good designers, product developers, and marketers—innovators of all stripes—must be able to address, whether their end users are making a simple cup of tea or managing their finances online.

In high-trust ecosystems, where the default set of expectations is that products and services will be trustworthy, the trust indicators fall along the lines of maintaining and upholding the trust that's already there, by way of authenticity, fulfillment, reliability, and recourse. TV ads pitch slogans like "Chevy Runs Deep," highlighting the brand's longstanding reputation rather than its new products and features.

For consumers in low-trust ecosystems, where the baseline is a lack of trust and vendors need to prove themselves trustworthy to potential customers, trust indicators are designed to pull those potential customers up from the zone of rejection into the zone of sufficient trust. These indicators tend to address the dimensions that have the most serious consequences when violated: safety and value. It's one thing to spend a month's wages on a mobile phone that turns out not to be the brand you think you're buying, but it's another thing entirely to spend a month's wages on a phone that can't actually make calls, or even worse, one that might electrocute you.

It doesn't take much to create a sniff test for these conditions, besides a little ingenuity. In Chongqing, China, where spitting in public is still a relatively common practice,* taxicabs generally use seat covers as trust indicators of cleanliness (that is, safety), and the most trustworthy ones are those that have the current day of the week printed on the backside of the front seat covers. That's not to say that drivers of other taxicabs aren't changing their seat covers every day, but they're not making the same effort to communicate directly to their clients and reassure them.

In parts of the world like Uganda and Afghanistan, where, as of 2009, only 9 percent and 15 percent of their respective populations had access to electricity, many mobile phone users go to market kiosks where vendors with a car battery or variable power supply offer to charge phones for a small fee. But how do customers know they won't be ripped off by a vendor whose battery is

---

* Spitting, especially when foreigners draw attention to it, is probably the one issue that creates more negative feedback from educated, cosmopolitan Chinese than any other, at least based on conversational feedback to this topic. To hazard a guess why: spitting serves a personal and very selfish function, and it naturally exposes others to whatever is spat. Spitting is also far more common in agrarian cultures where the physical activity of (dirty) manual labor is more likely to trigger spittable moments, and where, because of population density and natural surfaces (dirt and grass), the negative impact of spitting on others is generally lower than in urban settings. For the modern urban dweller, spitting is a close and uncomfortable reminder of where that society has come in a short space of time, of how life (and income levels and attitudes) used to be. In short: it's a marker for educated, cosmopolitan Chinese of what they want to leave behind. The grating is indicative of the tension between modern and traditional China, and the speed at which things are changing.

out of juice? In the off-grid markets of Afghanistan, vendors connect lightbulbs to their power supply, and those lit bulbs tell the trust-me story. And how do customers know their phones will be safe from thieves between drop-off and pickup times? At stalls in Uganda, I noticed that vendors stored phones in small lockers, which for all I know was little more than security theater, but like any form of security theater the intent was to offer peace of mind, not necessarily an ironclad guarantee against theft.

Sometimes service offerings build milk-sniffing opportunities directly into the design and mechanics of the service itself. Taobao, China's equivalent of eBay, operates in a low-trust ecosystem, arguably even less trustworthy online than it is in person. The biggest transactional difference between eBay and Taobao is that Taobao created a dedicated chat platform, so buyers and sellers can negotiate and sniff each other out in real time. Second, they allow customers to put payments into an escrow account until they've received the product and are satisfied with it. In essence, Taobao not only mediates business transactions, it also brokers trust relationships between buyers and sellers. These differences were among the reasons why eBay failed in China, and Taobao has emerged as the clear winner.

Of course, there are much more subtle ways to build trust into products and services. Design cues such as color, texture, typography, shape, size, volume, and weight all contribute to establishing trust that something will deliver on its promise.

The next time you're out shopping for anything from personal electronics to toothpaste, try the following thought exercise. Take a moment to look at two or three products within the same category and think about what makes you trust one more than the other(s). Is it the brand names? Your past experiences with the products? Is it in the design of the packaging? The price? Now consider the consequences of making the "wrong" choice, where there's a significant deficit between what you expected and what you ended up with. Would you feel ripped off? Ashamed of wasting your money? (And is that shame on you, your peer group, or even relative strangers such as the shop assistant?) Would you make an effort to share your newfound distrust? Is there any context or circumstance that could potentially amplify those consequences or mitigate them?

After evaluating these consequences, think about the relative price you're willing to pay for a trustier product. How much trust is enough, and how much would be overdoing it? How would you react to a product that significantly overengineered trust? What if, for instance, a six-pack of sponges was packaged as smartly as an upscale smartphone, or came with a warranty card that asked for your personal information, or promised that if anything went wrong with your sponges you could replace them in a jiffy at the brand's flagship store?

If you want to get deeper into this thought exercise, ask yourself how you would evaluate the trustworthiness of the products in question at each of the five stages in Beal and Bohlen's diffusion process from chapter 3—awareness, interest, evaluation, trial, and adoption—as well as beyond adoption, over the course of use.

Lastly, there's the matter of trust at the end of use, and the design elements that indicate when a product expires, wears out, or loses its efficacy. Like the student who sniffed his milk, we can sometimes rely on our senses to tell us when things have gone sour (not always quite so literally), and many built-in warnings add some sensory element, like the sound of car brakes' wear indicators or the smell added to natural gas to help us detect leaks. However, in instances where these mechanisms register as false positives, like expiration dates that fall well before food actually goes bad, or toothbrush indicator bristles that suggest replacing a still-functional brush, we lose our trust in the mechanisms themselves and start to ignore them. So, while you're comparing the trustworthiness of products, think about what sniff tests they offer, if any, and what it would take to not only build in these mechanisms, but also make them worth paying attention to.

We're all consumers. When we consider our own choices through this thought exercise we can gain insight into the rationales behind our consumption choices. For anyone trying to bring to market products and services that other people will trust enough to use, let alone love, a systematic approach to these questions is vital to understanding.

By now, it should be fairly obvious that trust affects, and is affected by, practically every aspect of the consumer environment, from the settings in which transactions take place to the brands behind the goods to the very design and presentation of the goods themselves. Hundreds of volumes have been written on the subject and countless more will be written yet, so my aim is not to diagram every facet of trust relationships for you, but to give you a few new angles from which to approach it. And I've saved one of the most puzzling yet fascinating strands for the end of this chapter: how entire marketplaces can be built on foundations of lying, cheating, and stealing—and thrive in spite of breaking the unwritten rules of trust.

The Rise of the Superfakes

Chengdu, the capital of Szechuan Province, is one of those Chinese megacities you rarely hear about, with a population over 14 million. On one wintry trip in 2006, I took the opportunity to explore the city with a fellow traveler by way of alleys and back-streets, and chanced across a gent who had set up the local equivalent of a sex shop: a small wooden trunk on the back of his motorbike, folded out to reveal a range of libido enhancers and condoms. Farther down the alley, we found two more ersatz shops set up in the same way. All of them sold locally produced libido enhancers, and their wares included a product purporting to be Viagra—shaped and sized like Viagra, in what appeared to be Viagra packaging.

In a low-trust ecosystem, the odds were high that the products on sale would not live up to their promise, compounded by the fact that the "stalls" were mobile (lowering opportunities for recourse should something go wrong). Yet there in that alley, three competing stalls all vied for the same trade—mostly middle-aged men looking for a rise. Chinese libido enhancers routinely oversell their properties ("lasts for 216 hours, good for the kidney"),* and by comparison the Viagra packaging was

---

* I ran a short follow-up study on the packaging of libido enhancers, this time from a market stall in Chongqing: http://hddn.ps/57-lessons-for -service-design.

modest: a white box with a contents sticker, with a logo on the side. The presence of three market stalls selling competing products suggested that there was a viable market for these products, even though the risk of buying a fake or a product that didn't live up to its promise was extremely high, including the potential cost of ingesting a harmful substance. Why would someone buy something where the risk of getting a fake was so high? Such behavior would seem to violate all the rules of trustworthiness we've just discussed.

And yet, according to the Organisation for Economic Co-operation and Development's latest report on counterfeiting and piracy, published in 2008, such products accounted for 1.95 percent of total global trade—somewhere in the neighborhood of $250 billion. These are just ballpark figures, of course—black markets are inherently difficult to reckon, since bootleggers don't release quarterly sales reports, not to mention the value discrepancies between things like digital copies of MP3s and reverse-engineered cars. The actual cost is tough to calculate as well, in real economic terms. After all, the marketplace wouldn't exist if it didn't benefit both buyers and sellers.

Over the past few years, Microsoft has been trying to tackle the issue of software piracy in China, from lawsuits against electronics stores that allegedly sold computers with pirated software preinstalled to investments in the city of Hangzhou, which Microsoft has hailed as "a showcase" for its promise to crack down on intellectual-property violators. In 2011, CEO Steve Ballmer proclaimed that the company's revenue in China amounted to only 5 percent of its revenue in the United States, despite similar personal-computer sales figures in the two countries. I don't know how he arrived at that number, but I can say anecdotally that if you walk a few blocks in almost any Chinese city, you'll probably be able to find a sidewalk vendor selling pirated Windows CDs for about 20 yuan (or $3).

However, even if Ballmer's claim is true, I'd argue that Microsoft actually benefited from counterfeiting. Although revenue may be relatively slim, the adoption of their products and platforms has created a culture of use. Pirated copies are both an awareness- and literacy-building exercise, which is especially valuable for something as technically challenging to the average user as a computer operating system. The time, money, and mental energy invested in learning one operating system, regardless of whether it's an authentic or pirated version, becomes a barrier to the adoption of an alternative operating system. It earns consumer loyalty, even if those consumers are not yet paying customers, or at least not yet paying the company that created the original product. The return for a company like Microsoft is that it earns a greater opportunity to turn the consumer of the faked product into a paying customer further down the line, whether selling access to a service through its online marketplace, or through its ecosystem partners' hardware.

Both the fake Viagra and the bootlegged Windows raise important and often confounding questions about trust. Looking at the Viagra from a consumer's perspective, why would someone trust a product that almost certainly falls short on authenticity and recourse, and poses very real risks in terms of safety, reliability, fulfillment, and value? First, when lacking alternatives, consumers are often willing to lower their trust thresholds. Brick-and-mortar sex shops, though more prevalent now, were virtually nonexistent in China in 2005. Second, Viagra is close to being an essential good; desperate consumers might be willing to assume more risk in order to reap its supposed benefits. Third, like so many other counterfeit goods from sneakers to mobile phones, fake Viagra presents an implicit tradeoff many consumers are willing to make—the cost in terms of risk versus the cost in terms of money. People who buy counterfeits like Viagra have a more abundant supply of risk-taking currency than financial currency.

That third answer may seem to make the most sense in terms of pure economic logic, but based on all the conversations I've had over the years with people situated at the bottom of the economic pyramid, I'd argue that they of all people can least afford to assume the risk of buying a product that doesn't live up to its promise, since they can least afford to replace it. They are some of the toughest customers around. They sometimes buy counterfeit goods knowing full well that they're phony, either because those are the only versions they have access to; because they care more about the brand values than the physical products themselves (not so much for Viagra, but certainly for things like Nikes and iPhones); or because they have to address immediate needs on limited budgets and can't afford the time it would take to save up for the genuine article. In China, we've seen consumers gradually shift from buying fakes to coveting (and sometimes buying) originals as their appreciation of the differences between the real and the fake rises.

The pirated software, or any other form of illegal digital copying, raises a whole other set of trust issues. While there may be some risk of viruses or malware, the general assumption is that the bootlegged products are perfect facsimiles of the originals. Consumers have about as much trust in the pirated version as they do in the real one, aside from the obvious recourse deficit since sidewalk vendors don't offer much in the way of customer service. The trust problems here are on the supply side, and the biggest question is not whether piracy can be eradicated through lawsuits or buddying up to authorities promising iron fists, but whether companies are better off investing in marginal antipiracy efforts—antipiracy theatrics as it were—or in developing new products and services that can still earn a profit despite being ripped off. This may seem like a question specifically for the music, film/TV, and publishing industries, whose business models have been upended by the digital revolution, but increasingly it's one for durable goods manufacturers as well.

China is again front and center in this matter, in part because it is the manufacturing hub of the world and by far the largest exporter of counterfeit and pirated goods (though only 15th out of 134 nations in exports of fakes relative to originals, according to the 2008 OECD report). Not only does China have an entire shadow industry devoted to copying and counterfeiting, but this industry—known as *shanzhai*, translated as "mountain fortress," but also derived from the word for "bandit"—has developed a culture of manufacturing and innovation around reverse-engineering *and then superseding* the genuine articles. Shanzhai manufacturers were the first to create mobile phones with multiple SIM card slots, a popular feature among users who subscribe to multiple networks in order to conserve minutes through free in-network calling. They were also the first to make phones with built-in electric shavers and cigarette storage compartments. Lest you think they only make handheld technologies, you might want to test-drive a shanzhai Porsche, or shop for some home furnishings at 11Furniture, which has replicated IKEA's products as well as their showrooms (sorry, no Swedish meatballs, though).

Though they won't admit it publicly, most global brands that manufacture in China see counterfeiting as something that comes with the territory. As one senior employee of a major athletic footwear company, speaking to the *New York Times* on condition of anonymity, remarked, "Does it cut into our business? Probably not. Is it frustrating? Of course. But we put it as a form of flattery, I guess."

There may not be reason to fear the knockoffs, but that doesn't mean shanzhai culture won't pose a serious threat to global brands. "Making counterfeit shoes is a transitional choice," one shanzhai factory manager told the *Times*. "We are developing our own brand now. In the longer term we want to make all our own brands, to make our own reputation." With a nimble network of manufacturers from every link in the supply chain, from the tiniest screw all the way up to the software platform, shanzhai producers can churn out complex electronic devices in a month that would ordinarily take a year to produce, often getting them to market before the so-called originals. What will happen when they take that ingenuity and run with it on their own? How will the corporations that used to outsource to these factories keep up? It may very well become a massive design and manufacturing revolution.

The question for Chinese consumers, then, is whom do you trust—the venerable brand you grew up with, or the no-name that was operating behind the scenes that whole time and has figured out how to deliver a better product at a better value? Whom do you buy from—the corporate, profit-driven brand that might encourage you to spend a bit more to buy into their brand values, or the shanzhai brand that's more driven to address consumer demand than profit motive? And in a global marketplace, it's not only a question for Chinese consumers— it's a question for all of us.

What if the answer was neither? What if you didn't have to choose between Ikea and 11Furniture, because instead of going out and buying a chair you could simply download the design scheme and 3-D-print it at home? If it seems far-fetched, consider that the controversial file-sharing website the Pirate Bay has already added a section of files for 3-D printing, and as the technology evolves over time it will surely become both more accessible and closer in quality to professional manufacturing processes.

So whom do you trust: the brand, the factory, or yourself? More important, whom do your potential customers trust? In which trust ecosystems will your products need to prove their worth? What are the cues that consumers use to ascertain trust? Which of those cues are culturally or contextually specific, and which apply across the globe? And with that in mind, how does this change what you bring to market? In a world of mistrust, how do you let consumers sniff the milk? You can find the guidelines within these pages, but it's up to you to ask yourself—and your potential customers—these contextually dependent questions if you want answers that truly give you confidence.

Chapter 7

Finding the Essence

Imagine yourself on the back of a motorbike taxi, buzzing through the scarred concrete streets of Ho Chi Minh City's outer residential neighborhoods on a sweltering June morning. You fix your gaze on the rows upon rows of TV antennas jutting from rooftops and contemplate their statement on status symbolism and technology adoption, until something at street level grabs your attention. It's not much: a large bottle containing three or four liters of semitransparent liquid, perched atop a brick, attended to by a kid, no more than ten years old, who holds a length of plastic tubing in his hand and watches to see if you'll stop. Your driver pulls over. You've arrived at the gas station— not just any gas station, but the very *essence* of a gas station.

Everything you take for granted in your typical gas station experience has been stripped away. All that's left is a bottle of fuel, sitting slightly higher than the fuel tank it aims to fill, a hose to transfer fuel from the container to the tank, and an agent for collecting payment. It's so rudimentary, and yet so pure—it would be impossible to take anything away and still have a functioning gas station.

When I came across this setup for the first time (I've since seen it in Indonesia, Tajikistan, and several other developing countries) it was startling enough to force me to unlearn everything I had assumed about something I'd long taken for granted—the gas station experience. When you peel back all the layers of the typical American (or Chinese or German or British) gas station—the towering branded sign shouting the price-per-gallon in foot-high numbers; cars sidled up against a half-dozen pumps and sheltered by a large, framelike canopy; an attendant tucked behind a thick layer of security glass; security cameras; the convenience store stocked with fresh coffee and an assortment of snacks; the dirty bathroom—what you're essentially left with is a bottle on a brick.

If you know what you're looking for, seeing something in its purest possible form is inspiring, but what does it mean to find the essence? How do you know what you're seeing? And what do you do with that "bottle-on-a-brick," so to speak, when you discover it?

We all grow accustomed to the world around us. Objects, as they become more familiar, blend into the landscape and once-novel practices that required forethought at every step become automatic. We stop asking questions because the answers, the ways things work, appear obvious, even when they're not—or when the origins of that obviousness are long forgotten.

But if we start stripping things back to the bare essentials, we can build or rebuild our understanding of services from the ground up. We can also take the same essence and use it as a starting point for designing variations of the same service for different markets, developed or developing, so that the front ends speak to the nuances of each market—to actual customers, on the ground, in their daily lives—while the back end leverages core processes and infrastructure.

One way to think of a road map of possibilities for a given product or service over time is as in the shape of a cone, starting from a clear point that marks the present and expands continuously into the future. And what could be more emblematic of such a simple starting point, unencumbered by assumptions, than a bottle-on-a-brick? With that simple image in mind, it becomes easier to explore any number of design directions.

The cone is only meant to suggest a theoretical range of options. Once you start heading down a specific design path and incorporate more and more options, you run the risk of falling into the trap known as "creeping featurism," a bad habit of adding more and more layers of functions and features that ultimately prove more bewildering than useful. Don Norman, in his influential book *The Design of Everyday Things*, describes creeping featurism as "a disease, fatal if not treated promptly," which can be cured with a heavy dose of organization, but "as usual, the best approach is to practice preventive medicine." John Maeda, the designer and now also president of the Rhode Island School of Design, preaches the mantra "simplicity equals sanity." In *The Laws of Simplicity*, Maeda sets down ten laws for designers to abide by, the first two being Reduce and Organize, which also happen to be Norman's proscribed cures for creeping featurism. Arguably, the best way to abide by those laws is to hew as closely as possible to the essence, and at the very least make sure that the essence isn't obscured by nonessential bells and whistles.

There are several ways to find the essence, all of which involve some form of mental reframing. In the design world, we talk about seeing products and services with "fresh eyes," bringing new perspectives to a project to get a different sense of what things are and what they could be. Fresh eyes can come when new members are injected into a team, but we can also refresh our own eyes by aiming them in new directions, and by using methods that force us to reevaluate what we have long since taken for granted.

Over the years I've found inspiration in highly resource-constrained communities (what you might call "poor," but of course poverty is relative), often in developing countries, but also in certain pockets of more developed ones. Let's take two examples: one from a reasonably well-off community in Kobra-sol, Brazil, and another from Ulaanbaatar, the capital of Mongolia. In the former, I once came across a photo booth that looks just like the kind you'd find in London, Tokyo, or Paris but with one notable omission—it doesn't include a camera. A photo booth without a camera might sound like an oxymoron, but it's actually nicely attuned to the local availability of resources. The core of the booth-oriented service is providing a standardized identity-card photo background, but the print shop in which the booth is located provides the camera for other services beyond simply taking booth-style passport photos. Over in Ulaanbaatar, I've found "mobile phone kiosks" that consisted of bulky landline-style desk phones (though not actually connected to landlines, as they were powered by battery and contained SIM cards) carried by a kiosk operator walking in step with her customer, resulting in a beautiful urban choreography where the customer was simultaneously mobile and tethered by the phone cord. While the desk phone form factor was very much of its time (2005), and many of these customers would now own their own mobile phone, the "mobile phone kiosk" service revealed the nuances of where the demand for the service was greatest, and allowed customers to walk and stay warm while making a call—Ulaanbaatar in midwinter is not the kind of place where you want to stand still outside for too long (but it's great for a Friday night out if you're ever in the neighborhood).

While the streets are great for scoping out leads and hunting for clues, we use a variety of techniques during research projects to complement this ground-level activity. The simplest is to systematically observe use; to ask questions around why people are doing things in a particular way. Almost every study involves spending significant time in people's homes, where they're most likely to do things "their way." Another is to track data on actual use. In more formal research settings, we also sometimes ask our participants to (figuratively) strip down a product or a service to its core reason for being. Participants are provided with a blank slate, and it's up to them to decide what features to include, provided that they can fit all their desired features into the "budget," which allows for somewhere between only one-third and one-half of the usual features. This exercise forces participants to think about which features they value most and how the ones they choose might interplay with one another, and it gives the research team a different kind of insight about consumer preferences than a simple list of features ranked from most to least important. Each approach carries its risks—for example, some people are better at articulating why they prefer one thing to another, and many people struggle to articulate forward-looking needs—but a skilled research team knows how to mitigate them and draw out the right kind of information and inspiration from each session.

Back in the office there are many other systematic ways to reframe what a service could be, using various stimuli to take the team in different directions. These are often presented through different lenses—for a project on banking this might include what security, convenience, or the notion of "good service" means to a bank's customers, or what their technological landscape looks like. The reasons why things are done in a particular way are often told through personalities (or personas, archetypes, or actual consumers that match a particular market segment), drawing on the rich firsthand field data. Processes such as buying gasoline, making a phone call, or even making a cup of tea can be mapped out step by step and reimagined. Frameworks (including the threshold framework) can be introduced to put findings into perspective and encapsulate what the team deems important.

A common workshop activity is to introduce lateral thinking exercises (such as those devised by Edward de Bono) that put the team and clients together in a room, incorporating a series of tasks to break down the team's preconceptions and forcing them to figure out how to integrate something completely incongruous into that picture. For example, we might be looking at a service like commercial banking, and our left-field stimulus could be a fluffy Chinese panda toy. We'd start by mapping out all the properties of the panda toy: color, texture, cultural implications, production quality, and some slightly tangential panda-related ideas like endangered species, artificial insemination, and the World Wildlife Fund (which uses a panda in its logo). Then we'd move on to mapping the attributes of commercial banking, and then brainstorm how to work in panda attributes in some way. The starting point might be the iconic form of the panda, but the discussion might move to figuring out what the banking equivalent of artificial insemination could be.

Building a process around this sort of essence-level brainstorming provides structure for creative ideation, which for most people is extremely difficult unless they're able to escape the constraints of their assumptions. It's a process of deconstruction and reconstruction, and it can lead to some wild, fun, and most likely impractical ideas. But it can also lead to some that seem like common sense—the kinds of ideas that might be way off your radar and yet make you say, "Why didn't I think of that?" Those insights tend to be the ones that capture the essence better than any of the others. A guy in a panda suit greeting customers as they walk into a bank is an obvious idea but not a commonsense one. On the other hand, giving bank customers tools to make sure their money is safe, anytime and anywhere, so that they feel as secure as a child cuddling a big plush panda— that's about as close to the essence of banking as you can get. While this level of cuteness might grate on your mental model of what you want from a banking service, in countries such as South Korea or Japan it's simply run-of-the-mill.

The Gas Station, sans Gas

Imagine you're an alien visiting earth for the first time and you come across an English soccer match in progress; how would you describe it to your fellow aliens? One very simple way to describe the scene was that twenty-two people were chasing a pig's bladder around a patch of grass.

The value of this exercise is not just to show how things could be misconstrued when they become abstracted to a certain point, but also what sorts of ideas and assumptions can come of building up from that point of abstraction. If twenty-two people were chasing a pig's bladder around a field, perhaps the central objective might be to kick it into a net, but it might also be to capture it and destroy it. Or the objective might be to annoy the odd-looking twenty-third man, dressed in black, whose tortured role is underlined by his occasional piercing and obviously painful whistle. Or, in a society where gardening is elevated to religion, the purpose is to aerate and sear the sacred grass using slaves wearing specially designed boots.

As a design exercise, the process of stripping something down to its core is wonderfully rewarding in itself, and perhaps the completely stripped-down version presents a striking elegance that could offer unique value in the marketplace. But the deeper understanding of that core comes in the reconstruction, especially when you consider how a product or service would fundamentally change if something else were at the core.

What would happen if the essence of a gas station weren't a bottle on a brick, but some currently peripheral aspect of the experience? Say you're an alien checking out a gas station for the very first time: watching people pull in, head inside the convenience store, browse for a bit, stand in line to pay, and then at the last moment make impulse purchase decisions. What if your assumption was that the whole experience was created to trigger impulse-purchasing behavior?

If that were the case, think about how the whole station might be built up from that focal point. Queues could be carefully orchestrated so that every customer had to wait long enough to be properly exposed to tempting goods on display within arm's length of the queuing area, but not so long that they would leave out of frustration. Gas could simply be bait for larger purchases—for every gallon you buy you get an extra percentage discount on a new TV or dream vacation.

What if the core function of a gas station were to facilitate dating? The design of the forecourt could facilitate interaction between potential partners, with clear lines of sight between customers to check out each other (and each other's vehicle). The gas-filling process could provide enough waiting time to strike up a conversation, but not so much that customers were committed to a dud interaction. Attractive attendants could provide services like washing windshields, checking oil and other lubricating fluids, inflating tires, and bringing snacks and beverages to customers. The end of the process might provide a natural way to transition to somewhere a little more intimate. Will there be a point where the gifting of gasoline is considered the universal sign of affection, akin to chocolates or diamonds?

What if the gas station were based around a concept of being a specialty purveyor of fine all-hours food? Or the best bathroom in town? Or even something radically different from the current setup, like an art gallery or an amusement park?

The point of the exercise is not to try to come up with the most ridiculous concept, or to skip past the ridiculous ones and focus on the ones closest to the current core, but to understand how each nonessential layer repositions the whole experience. It can also give you some sense of how a person with no need for the core function might think about the experience. For someone who needs to use the bathroom and walks past a gas station, a bottle of gasoline on a brick won't do them any good, but if the station were designed in a decidedly different way, he might be tempted to make an impulse purchase (or use a dating service).

The other value in the exercise is to reconsider the core in light of the introduction of a new technology or standard. Consider that at the turn of the twentieth century, gasoline was sold by pharmacies as a niche product for the few people wealthy enough to own cars, and who were also typically wealthy enough to employ drivers who could maintain those cars. As more and more middle-class Americans became car owners, service stations popped up across the country, offering what we now think of as "full service," administered by attendants who would pump fuel, check oil and other fluid levels, inflate tires, and offer any mechanical assistance needed. "Service" was really the operative term, and the essence of the experience. Major chains like Texaco and Gulf advertised the friendliness of their attendants, and lured customers with free road maps as part of their brand promise: to help drivers get where they needed to go.

As cars became more reliable and thus required less frequent maintenance, and new technologies made it safe for drivers to pump their own gas and allowed them to pay electronically, the essence shifted away from service to refueling—not only for cars but for drivers as well, with convenience stations offering snacks, beverages, cigarettes, and restrooms.

Although both the "service" and "pit stop" paradigms offer far more than a bottle-on-a-brick, they could each be considered the essence of a gas station within their respective contexts, because they provide additional services that have become virtually essential aspects of the business. Of course, what passes for necessity in one place doesn't always travel well around the world.

For instance, after the Japanese government deregulated gas stations in 1998 to allow self-service, many drivers refused to make the switch from full service, or did so with great trepidation. "I'm afraid I'll set the place on fire," one Japanese mother of two told the *Los Angeles Times* as an attendant coached her and other drivers shortly after the switch. Even a decade after deregulation, only 16 percent of all gas stations in Japan were self-service, and the Japan Automobile Federation continued to receive requests for help from drivers whose cars had broken down because they had mistakenly pumped the wrong type of fuel.*

As for American "pit stop" gas stations, which have struggled in recent years—since 1991, when there were almost 200,000 stations in the United States, more than 50,000 of them have shuttered, according to the National Association of Convenience Stores—profits from sales of gas are hard to come by, so

---

* The issue of putting the wrong type of gasoline into the tank has largely been solved through the use of pump nozzles that can only fit into the appropriate type of tank.

snacks and drinks are indispensable to keep the remaining stations afloat. The owner of one particularly famous station in Washington, D.C., has even adopted a particularly distorted market strategy: jacking his gas prices sky-high, sometimes a dollar more per gallon than the station across the street. Why? "He doesn't want to sell much gasoline," Dan Gilligan, the president of the Petroleum Marketers Association of America, told the *Washington Post*.

Still, as long as people keep driving automobiles, they'll need to get their juice somewhere. But, going forward, will the "pit stop" remain at the core of the refueling/recharging experience, even as more and more cars run on electricity instead of (or in addition to) gasoline? The predominant model for public charging so far, putting chargers next to parking spaces, has been much closer to the bottle-on-a-brick than the pit stop. Since electricity doesn't require a large underground tank and pumps (a minimally accoutered charging stall needs only a few square feet of real estate, no more than a phone booth), it's easier to distribute large numbers of these "stations" around cities rather than at select intersections. We may also see more centralized stations that offer battery swapping, a rapid alternative to the twenty- to thirty-minute process of recharging a car battery, but one that requires more infrastructure to warehouse and charge larger numbers of batteries. In High Falls, New York, in the Hudson River valley, a reclamation project is renovating an abandoned gas station and converting it into a charging station, yoga studio, and wellness center. At what point do gas stations go the way of phone booths, or, to a lesser extent, traditional Main Street banks?

It seems like charging a vehicle in the city may simply become an incidental aspect of stopping and parking while doing something else, like shopping or dining. But what about highway travel? What will be the essence of a charging station out on the open road? Will station owners have to build in experiences, perhaps miniature theme parks or video arcades, to keep their customers entertained while waiting? There are nearly infinite possibilities for what they may be able to do, but the opportunity lies in figuring out what their customers can't do without.

Building an Un-Frastructure

If you're willing and able to read this book, I'd venture to guess that you have at least one bank account, most likely more than one, with myriad ways of accessing your money, from debit cards to ATMs, a checkbook to a mobile banking app. Once most people have access to this level of service they don't spend very much time thinking about what they like about it, much less thinking about the essence of what it offers them. At its core, banking is about keeping it somewhere safe until it needs to be retrieved, and being able to transfer that money to others wherever they are. Needless to say, losing all of your (or your family's) money is a threat to survival, but that threat is primarily felt by people who don't have access to these fundamental services.

This is precisely the kind of notion that clients in the financial services and banking space like to explore, to challenge their own idea of what a bank is and does. Unfortunately they often lack a sense of how to reset assumptions and build something fresh that still addresses the core motivations driving customers to hand their money over to banks.

For many people living in developed countries, banking is woven tightly into the fabric of their lives and culture, so it can be hard to fathom what it means to lack access to banking and what the pain points of "banklessness" look like. It's also difficult to study in our own backyards, without taking the highly unethical step of taking away people's existing access and asking them to try surviving without financial services. To see beyond the obvious, we have to travel to places where making a withdrawal literally means reaching under the mattress for a wad of cash.

The gap between developed and developing countries in terms of access to financial services is striking: about 49 percent of households around the world have deposit accounts, but that ranges from close to 100 percent in Japan to less than 1 percent in the Democratic Republic of the Congo and Afghanistan. Access is growing, but the numbers don't always add up to significant gains. For instance, from 2008 to 2009, the nation of Burundi (population 8 million) doubled the total number of ATMs across the country—*from 2 to 4* (using an ATM as a signifier of more formal banking services). In contrast, Canada, with the highest concentration of ATMs per capita, had about one for every 458 adults. But regardless of nationality, people are driven by the same basic motives when it comes to their money. The difference is that, in a place like Canada, if you ask someone why he puts his money into bank accounts, he might say, "Because that's where it goes," whereas if you ask a Burundian with no bank account why he sews his money into the lining of his coat, his response is paradoxically more likely to tell you about the essence of banking: he wants his money to be safe, until the very moment that he needs it.

If you asked a Brit or an American forty years ago what a quintessential bank looked like, you would hear descriptions of marble floors and thirty-foot-high ceilings, velvet-roped queues and tellers behind windows, big vaults and the big gentlemen in pin-striped suits who had access to those vaults. Today the architecture is more unassuming, but the idea of a bank, to its customers, is less about the branch and more about the ATMs, the online services, and increasingly mobile apps. None of that, however, is really at the core. It still is, as it always was, about safety and access. All that infrastructure is just the shell, and it follows the same metaphor of technology adoption and abandonment that we see in other realms: we are all hermit crabs, wherever we live and whatever we do, and we inevitably migrate from one shell to another when we find one that better suits our needs.

As we learned in chapter 4, safety and access mean different things to different people. For those who value tangibility as the only guarantor of something's existence, there will always be a need for secure containers of money, whether they use vaults or mattresses. For others who put their faith in zeroes and ones, a line on a computer screen that tells someone she has $20,000 to her name is enough to make her feel like she and she alone is in possession of those $20,000. A bank can wrap any type of shell it can fathom around that essential core of safety and access, as long as it's a shell that dutifully encapsulates that core.

And in some cases it's not even a shell—at least not a physical one. Take, for instance, mobile money transfer services, such as M-Pesa in Kenya, that rely entirely on mobile networks and people networks rather than the more traditional physical banking infrastructure. With M-Pesa, consumers can sign up for an account through their mobile phone, and deposit or withdraw funds through agents in much the same way as they were buying and "transferring" prepaid airtime, as discussed in the story from Uganda in the introduction. Simple, a web-based service that issues payment cards, allows deposits through smartphones and withdrawals through ATMs, money transfers, and bill payments. And yet, as their site proclaims, "Simple is not a bank. Simple replaces your bank." It has no branches, no vaults, no tellers, and no lines, but it is FDIC-insured. Before it even launched, Simple had more than 100,000 prospective customers who had requested to be put on its waiting list. It works because it attends to the essence of what people want for their money, built from the ground up using today's dominant mode of technology, and with the promise of transparency regarding fees.

The idea of stripping away banking's infrastructure and getting down to its essence of safety and access opens up a huge cone of possibilities, and makes for a good thought exercise about the ups, downs, and tradeoffs involved in what could be. What if we could access banking services (or certain aspects of banking) at any sort of networked access point? Instead of through ATMs and cash registers, why not connect with your bank account through transit fare ticket machines? What if every vending machine in the city could serve as a summary display for your bank account details, like the Tokyo vending machines that display your account balance? What if every point-of-sale terminal were your printer, and not only printed receipts but whatever sort of data you wanted? (Again using the Tokyo transit system as an example, the ticket machines that top up transit cards can also print out records of any given card's use by date, time, and location.) Or what if every point-of-sale terminal was an ATM? And what if every mobile phone was a point of sale? What would it take for you to be able to turn to the next person in line (whom you've never met before) and have them pay?

The Cone of Possibility, the Cone of Opportunity

When it comes to the actual task of finding the essence of a product or service and then building new possibilities, start-ups have a natural advantage. After all, no one can reasonably expect their local gas station to tear out all the pumps, the tank, and the convenience store and replace everything with a massive bottle perched atop a massive brick (tempting though it may be). The sunk costs of existing infrastructure can greatly narrow the cone of possibility, but it may also narrow the cone of opportunity, especially when customers are ready to change shells before a business is.

Start-ups also possess the power to tickle the imagination, especially for the techno-optimists out there who see utopia on the other side of today's frontier. There is no shortage of dreamers, like the libertarian "seasteaders" who want to create brandnew, self-ruling cities, set afloat in international waters where existing governments can't infringe on their ideas (or their pocketbooks).

But there are also plenty of cautionary tales from new ventures that set out to capture the absolute purest possible essence of something, only to strip away a bit too much and miss the mark. For example, we can look back now on the rollout of the Tata Nano, which promised to revolutionize car ownership by developing the absolute cheapest possible car in the world. What the makers of the Tata Nano failed to realize was that the essence of car ownership is not just four wheels and an engine, but also the social status conferred by being a car owner—which in the Nano's case was the stigma of being seen as the owner of the cheapest car in the world.

And while up-and-running ventures lack the wide range of possibilities inherent in start-ups, they have the not-to-be-underestimated advantage of experience. Past success, while no means an indicator of future results, is usually a sign that beneath all the accumulated layers of features and widgets and amenities lies a legitimate understanding of essence. There's nothing wrong with a gas station that offers far more than a bottle-on-a-brick. But in order to understand the value of those additional layers, and find out what opportunities lie in adding or subtracting them from the equation, it's quite useful to imagine peeling each one away to see whether its absence indeed makes the heart grow fonder or whether it's just dead weight.

If simplicity is akin to sanity, finding the essence is not a wholesale brainwash, but rather a reality check.

Chapter 8

The Great Tradeoff

It is probably the world's most underrated conundrum, faced by tens of millions of people every day. Make the right choice and a timely ablution waits; make the wrong choice and receive minor embarrassment, discomfort, and quite possibly a haranguing from a member of the opposite sex. Our near-universal competence in making the right choice is a testament to our ability to draw on our understanding of how the world works, taking in and processing an array of visual, audio, tactile, and olfactory cues, and to translate the stimuli into that all-important decision: choosing the proper door to enter for either the men's or the ladies' room.

Public restrooms may not immediately spring to mind when you think about designing user experiences, but in fact they serve as valuable examples of the power that all kinds of designers and innovators wield in altering the tone of everyday people's lives, for ease and comfort but also (typically unintentionally) for vexation and shame.

Public restrooms provide an invaluable service, as they're used throughout the world by a wide swath of population across all ages, genders, ethnicities, and levels of income, education, and literacy. For some, a public toilet is a last resort; for others, it's the only option aside from finding a patch of land to squat over. Everyone needs to go at some point, and when you gotta go, you gotta go. And when you gotta go, as you approach those two doorways, the line between relief and humiliation can be as thin as the paint on the signs that distinguish ladies' from men's.

Stand in front of the toilets in Bangalore's century-old City Market at the end of the day and you'll find your senses assaulted. Aside from the natural decomposition of vegetables and flowers under the intense summer heat, you'll be faced with the collective pungency of urine from hundreds of market-goers, mainly emanating from one side of the building (peeing men tend to miss the toilet bowl or hole more than women do, and the scent lingers). Even if you've never stood in this spot before, the smell wafting out of the building would be enough to suggest its purpose as a public lavatory. As you might expect, there are other clues to what goes on inside: the words *gents* and *ladies* in English to the right of each door, and their Hindi equivalents

पुरुश and महिलाएँ

to the left. You'll also see large painted pictures of a smart, blue-shirted, mustachioed man and a sari'ed woman along with the names by each door. You could also draw on a lifetime's worth of experience vis-à-vis the use of public toilets in other locations, or the observation that men are streaming in and out of one door and women the other. All in all it's a rich environment, with each layer of contextual clues reinforcing the next. But we've all been in situations where the contextual clues that we would normally use to make the decision were missing.

A few years ago I was at a truck stop several hours outside of Tehran, my driver was sitting out front ordering tea that would in the end contain more sugar than water, and I was out back trying to find the restroom—or rather to decide which one was for me. One door was marked " آقایان " and the other " ها خانم." There was no color coding or iconography; the smell emanating from each room was the same subtle disinfectant; even poking my head through each door yielded nothing—just an identical view of a sink, flowers in a vase, and a row of blue-doored cubicles. Most men get reassurance from seeing a row of urinals, but these were missing—in Iran the government has mandated squatting as the position of choice for ablutions, with the side benefit of far less odor from pee-splash, thus leaving out another subtle cue. I flipped a mental coin, made my choice, and walked in. On the way out I noticed a stocky gent walking out the other door.

I had taken a fifty-fifty shot and missed, but all my guesswork could have been easily resolved if someone had simply placed masculine and feminine pictograms (or just masculine, given the cultural norms about depicting the female form) on the doors. However, the restroom door is a relatively simple design challenge, and most other products and services require far more complex operations than simply choosing which door to go through. Consider how many steps go into shopping online, booking a flight, printing a photo, or setting a washing machine for delicates, and consider how the choices that go into those steps rely on cues designed into the process itself, rather than from the world around it.

A great deal of effort goes into thinking about what kinds of people are likely to want to use, consume, or interact with a particular product or service, and what they want (and don't want) out of that experience. It's possible to make a product like a laptop or mobile phone virtually indestructible, but if the extra materials that go into its construction add to its cost, especially its cost relative to competing products, then consumers must make a tradeoff between cost and durability—and any tradeoff for consumers becomes a tradeoff for the people who design, build, and market the thing. If it's a product that consumers will quickly outgrow, or they plan to throw it away after a few uses, you could argue that devoting design resources to durability would make it a suboptimal design. Money spent on making it super-robust could be used on improving other aspects like screen resolution or weight, or could be saved in order to lower the cost of the device, dropping it into the price range of a wider range of consumers.

In a world where a single product such as a mobile phone could potentially sell in the tens if not hundreds of millions—the iPhone, for instance, sold more than 72 million units in 2011 alone—how do you know when to design something that works pretty well for everyone, something that works great for a subset of people, or something that works perfectly for only a handful?

And how do you deal with the ethical ramifications of catering to some people at the expense of others?

For instance: should a mobile phone manufacturer develop a special phone specifically optimized to be easy for illiterate people to use? It's a hypothetical question, with a great deal of emphasis on the "should" and "optimized" ends of it, but one that I was tasked to investigate for Nokia in 2005, after it had puzzlingly begun to see its phones bought by illiterate people who, by most definitions,* shouldn't have been able to use them.

At the time, Nokia was selling more than a quarter billion phones per year, and one in every three phones sold worldwide. Every one of those phones was designed with alphanumeric interfaces for people who could read and write, but many of them were being used by people who couldn't, resulting in a suboptimal user experience. Many of those phones were models like the iconic Nokia 3100: a simple, blockish handset with a black-and-white screen. Years earlier, the talk in the industry was that this type of phone would quickly fall into extinction as users in developed markets migrated to color screens and other bells and whistles. And yet that model had become the dominant growth engine for the company (as well as others, like telecoms, in the mobile ecosystem), delivering functionality at a price point that was acceptable to a broad spectrum of consumers in emerging

---

* The original 1958 UNESCO definition of literacy: "a person is literate who can with understanding both read and write a short simple statement on his or her everyday life, and can apply this knowledge to function in a textual environment."

markets—not just wealthy people in those markets, but even those on the bread (or rice) line.

Nokia owned the market for entry-level phones not only because they offered the right products but also because they had made an early investment in an incredibly strong distribution network, which proved critical in countries such as India, where 70 percent of the population lives outside urban centers. You could head out into pretty much any village and find Nokia phones for sale, perched atop sacks of rice and beans in small trading stations. The upshot of this success was that Nokia's products were being used in ways and places far beyond initial expectations, and in the process reached the consumer segment at the very base of the economic pyramid—an uncharted territory for most technology companies. And at that base, of course, illiteracy levels are the highest. Yet, surprisingly (to us, at least), illiteracy didn't necessarily prevent people from buying and using mobile phones.

When Suboptimal Is Optimal

Illiteracy is a challenging and beguiling puzzle. Some people and organizations consider it to be a disease that demands eradication, and yet it's a condition that we are all born into and one that will, by the very nature of how we develop over a lifetime, continue to exist. But the notion of illiteracy, and what it means to be a literate or illiterate person, also has a deep and fundamental impact on the relationship between people and the things they use in their everyday lives.

While there are very many definitions of literacy, the most common definition refers to *textual* literacy: the ability to read and write. Literacy, like most other skills, sits on a continuum ranging from totally illiterate to highly literate. The benefits of literacy tend to kick in when a person is able to apply that knowledge in a textual environment, whether reading signs in a marketplace or navigating a phone interface. Taking one step back, literacy can also be defined as a capacity to derive meaning from symbols or symbolic stimuli (after all, letters and words are but symbols). Textual literacy and numeracy (arithmetical literacy) are both extremely valuable skill sets for functioning in an information-based society, and as such they're critical components of schooling. However, people also develop other forms of literacy through unstructured learning and life experience, such as visual literacy, deriving meaning from how things look; observational literacy, deriving meaning from how people and things behave; tactile literacy, deriving meaning from how things feel; and aural literacy, deriving meaning from how things sound. The extent to which we are able to function in a given environment often depends on how well we apply a combination of these skills.[*]

Illiteracy is, arguably, fundamental to the human condition, in that every single person lacks at least some amount of knowledge that other people possess, and every deficit of knowledge comes with the cost of being unable to perform certain tasks

---

[*] On that note, I'd like to thank my coresearchers over the years, including Zeenath Hasan, Fumiko Ichikawa, and Yanqing Cui.

without assistance. Nobody is expected to know everything. Everyone is illiterate in some regard.

There are also moments when otherwise literate people function as if they were temporarily illiterate: when we forget, or we're distracted, or we're tired, or for any other reason that could cut off our ability to apply our mental capacity to something that requires some form of literacy. In that sense, a person walking across a street with a phone in hand is inherently partially sighted: either she's looking at the screen or she's looking at the vehicular and pedestrian traffic, but either way she's blind to one of those. Just as we are all blind at some point, we are all deaf, we are all paralyzed, and equally we're all illiterate. We are especially illiterate when it comes to cross-cultural understanding, most obviously because of language barriers, but also with regard to cultural practices.

The literacy gap can be overcome by any number of strategies people employ, not necessarily involving actual learning. One such strategy is *proximate literacy*—essentially asking more literate people for help. Many would consider this a form of dependence, but another way to look at proximate literacy is as a form of entrusting certain tasks to literate friends, relatives, or helpful strangers. In this sense, the strategy for some of the poorest members of society is the same as for some of the wealthiest: delegation.

Imagine an illiterate farmer needing to send a text message to a relative in the city, along with some instructions about sending money for a dowry and the timing of the wedding. Even if the farmer was sufficiently motivated to learn by rote how to open and send a new text message (to navigate the phone's interface, that is), he would struggle with editing the message, which would require an understanding of how the letters go together to form words (or, in a text message, abbreviations), and how to meaningfully string those words together into sentences with grammar appropriate to the receiver. Even if it were sent, there would be limited certainty that the message was received or understood. In this context, the strategy of asking for help makes complete sense: the farmer may not be literate, but within his social network he knows and relies on at least a few people who are. These people may not be nearby at the moment he needs one of them, so it might take hours or days to send the message. Also, because the person typing it in would be privy to the content of the message, it may take longer to find an appropriate person who can both assist and be trusted to "overhear" sensitive information. In communities with high levels of illiteracy, there is greater demand for this sort of assistance, and the practice of proximate literacy is considered more socially acceptable.

The Nokia study on illiteracy and mobile phone use turned out to be quite extensive, and the research on proximate literacy ultimately made it clear that a phone designed for illiterate users would have to be reframed to take into account this wider sense of competence. Put simply, what could users achieve by themselves *or* with support from others? And how did they decide what strategies to employ to be able to do the things that they wished to do? If the only thing a user wanted to do was receive calls, then "all" he needed to learn was how to keep the phone charged with power and airtime (the latter task often completed by the airtime seller), and to press the correct button when it rang. If his motivation was to make calls, he obviously needed to master the basics of navigating a phone menu, including how to retrace steps if there were errors, and how to recognize and type in numbers (often matching the number shapes on the keypad with the number shapes on his scrap-of-paper address book).

Another surprise finding in the research was that there were consumers who were literate in a particular language, such as Hindi, but were using a mobile phone whose interface did not support that language (even if there were other devices available on the market that supported their language). To understand what this entailed, think about whether you would use a highly desirable, high-value object like a mobile phone or car if its interface was in a language you didn't understand, rather than an alternative object that was less desirable but had a more comprehensible interface. In some contexts it would be fine to choose the easier-to-use option, but in others you'd generate significantly more social capital by being seen with the more prestigious status symbol.

The research conclusion was that it was better to continue selling more of the phone models that were already on the market, with a few subtle but important user interface tweaks, than to develop something wholly new and fully optimized for the specific needs of this particular consumer segment. The barrier of difficulty that we once assumed would overwhelm illiterate consumers was actually as surmountable as the extent to which they were able to tap their extended social networks and the occasional stranger for help. Using the existing phone, albeit with assistance, was more important than having it optimized for their special needs.

There were many other reasons why developing a dedicated product for illiterate consumers was not appropriate at that time. The social stigma associated with buying a device perceived as being designed for "disadvantaged" consumers would be a disincentive to purchase;[*] illiterates wanted the same device that everyone else had, because they aspired to be treated like everyone else. Furthermore, the costs of designing and testing a new device, getting it into supply channels, and educating sales and marketing teams versus the economies of scale of selling a few hundred million more of those that were already on the market risked making the price to consumers prohibitive. An optimized device would not necessarily have made a genuine difference in the lives of the people we initially thought it might help.

Although that outcome stuck in the craw of purists and ideologues who believed that such a device really would have been life-changing, the reality was that a notionally suboptimal device was good enough, and even superior to one that could have been engineered and designed better but at the risk of missing bigger-picture issues: a higher price tag, lowered social status, and the not-insignificant inconvenience of learning a new product.

---

* One of the better examples of appealing to "disadvantaged" consumers is the Japanese mobile operator DoCoMo's Raku-Raku series of phones designed for the elderly. The first versions, with a highly simplified interface, big buttons, large typefaces, and support for a physical address book, performed poorly in the marketplace, but when the designs shifted so that the phones appeared on the surface to look like most other devices on the market (while still sporting usability features geared toward elderly consumers), they became some of the top sellers.

Still, if I were asked to pursue the same question today, my answer may well be different. Many of these illiterate consumers are now on their third, fourth, or fifth phones, so they're well versed in learning to use new interfaces. Connectivity is both more reliable and faster, which makes the learning process more consistent. The cost of devices is now significantly lower: companies like Huawei and Nokia are increasingly putting touch-screen technology in the hands of lower-income consumers in emerging markets. Those touch-screen devices enable direct manipulation, rather than text inputs and menu navigations, making more complex tasks easier for an illiterate person to accomplish. And voice recognition technology has improved greatly, which means a nontextual interface that can recognize much more varied and nuanced language inputs, so we're closer to being able to talk to devices and have them talk back.

In hindsight, the illiteracy study offers a valuable example of the importance of timing, as well as the pitfalls of deep-rooted assumptions about consumers and their lives. The organizational assumption at that time (if anyone can truly speak for a geographically distributed organization the size of a small town) was that illiterate consumers would want to buy a phone designed for illiterate consumers. There was a time before the study when mobile phones were still considered luxury items for the wealthy, and we thought it would be crass to try to foist them on the people at the bottom of the economic pyramid—that the poor wouldn't be able to afford mobile phones or have much use for them. Hundreds of millions of low-income consumers have proved that assumption wrong.

Some people have wondered whether it was an ethical failure to pay minimal attention to bottom-of-the-pyramid consumers in the earlier days of mobile phones. Would it have been an ethical failure if we had built a phone for illiterate users without first evaluating whether they wanted or needed one? In both cases I would say no, but the reality is that the best way to do right by the people on the other end of the transaction is to understand how they tackle their own problems, rather than presuming to know how to solve those problems for them.

The idea of an "optimally" designed product has its allure, but optimal for whom and for what purpose? Optimal could mean faster, cheaper, lighter, higher quality, or more robust in any number of areas. And given that there's more than one notion of optimality, how do you reconcile the differences? And who gets to decide?

We're all inherently bounded in our perspectives by various -centricities: ethnocentricity, egocentricity, maybe even a bit of eccentricity. As hard as we try to understand new contexts and the people who live within them, it's easy to miss a beat, particularly coming at it from within a large corporation. Something that doesn't seem optimal from a developed-world perspective might be optimal from a developing-world perspective, especially when it comes to cost, which for many people living on the margins is the ultimate optimizer. What might seem like a nuisance to someone of means is often a clever (and sometimes necessary) method of cutting down the cost of use, such as skirting text message charges by placing a call and hanging up before the person on the other end answers.

Designers, problem solvers by nature, are additionally bounded by the "solutions mode" mentality. Always wanting to make things better has its altruistic qualities, but it can also come off as arrogant when a designer fails to respect the solutions that already exist, particularly those that have evolved from within a community.

A local solution may be the best solution, but it's not always a workable one, especially when it comes to things that require a complex supply chain, such as mobile phones and cars that can't necessarily be designed and manufactured locally in every part of the world. But even the corporations that make those sorts of global products owe it to themselves to understand what "local" actually means in the locales where they distribute their wares. The consequences of not understanding are very real. Contrary to what some humanitarian-minded thinkers are inclined to believe, it's the corporations, not the citizens of the developing world, who stand to lose more from their ignorance.

The Real Imperialism

It doesn't take much effort to find something about globalization to be incensed about: Starbucks pricing your favorite coffee shop out of the neighborhood; riots in Indonesia triggered by the Asian financial crisis; Apple imposing its corporate values by restricting the worldwide availability of adult content on their application platform; Coke and Pepsi logos being painted onto remote, pristine mountain ranges.

Or perhaps you prefer to take the profit-at-any-cost argument to the next level: Nestlé's aggressive sale of milk powder in markets where doing so is likely to inhibit the lactation of mothers; Facebook and Google endlessly redefining privacy in their race to monetize your personal information through new services; Monsanto's development of sterile seeds to force farmers to make repeat purchases every year; the very prominent suicide rate at Foxconn factories in China; Ericsson profiteering from the sale of monitoring equipment in countries like Iran; and accusations of racism in the advertising of Unilever's Fair & Lovely Skin Whitening creams. Make no mistake— governments, corporations, organizations, and agencies need to be monitored, held to account, and, in many markets where certain players hold a disproportionate amount of power, kept in check.

But as consumers, employers, and employees, I/you/we/they are complicit in this relationship in the products we make and consume, in the lifestyles we aspire to, and in the moment-to-moment decisions we make in how the products we buy are used. Sure, we demand privacy, but we are willing to let personal ethics slide when a photo opportunity presents itself. We have grown accustomed to free email but (momentarily) rally against our email being read by an algorithm so that Google can serve us more contextualized advertising. We roll up to a remote mountain village and mutter expletives when a ringtone goes off, but get the jitters at the mere thought of giving up our own connectivity. We complain of global warming and then jet off to another conference that espouses, among other things, sustainable living. We are highly vocal about the price of new electronics, but vote with our wallets when it comes to disposing of them in a slightly more costly but environmentally less harmful manner.

Or, we fly halfway around the world to conduct business, but we don't track every source of income that enables that business, or the many different players in the global network that allows us to get there, stay there, and communicate with collaborators and loved ones during our stay.

I spend a fair amount of time speaking and giving talks around the world, everywhere from corporate conferences to grammar schools. I'm always grateful for the opportunity to share and learn from the intellect in the room. But on occasion I'm confronted with accusatory questions that suggest that my work, or any sort of corporate presence in the developing world, is an outright scourge. This line of questioning typically stems from passionate minds, but also from misconceptions about consumers in highly income- and resource-constrained (in other words, poor) communities. Often these distortions are born from good intentions, but too often they stem from a failure to see people as they are, rather than as observers would like them to be. The list looks something like this:

- Consumers living on very low levels of income are incapable of making rational or the "right" choices for themselves, and need to be protected from corporations trying to hoodwink them.

- These consumers are bound by duty to only make rational choices. (In this case "rational" refers to those things that have an immediate benefit to their current socioeconomic situation, as defined by the person making the argument. For example, that it's okay to spend money on medicine for a sick kid, but not on electricity that allows that sick kid to watch TV.)

- Any time a consumer makes an "irrational" choice the "fault" lies with the company providing the products.

- Companies that target consumers in countries with very low levels of income are inherently evil.

When confronted by these sorts of arguments, I respond by pointing out that very-low-income consumers are—out of necessity, if nothing else—some of the world's most critical consumers. Only a small percentage of the world's population has the luxury of not having to think about every single thing they spend money on, the opportunity costs of buying one thing while forgoing others, and the social debts they might have to incur or collect in order to get by. Consumers with very low incomes are consistently pushed to make more rational choices than their wealthier counterparts because their day-to-day decision-making processes are more likely to revolve around how to carefully spend, and not misspend, their money. Like their wealthier counterparts, they also have inventive strategies for coping with limited and variable forms of income and credit, both formal and informal.

These sorts of tradeoffs are explored in the highly influential book *Portfolios of the Poor: How the World's Poor Live on $2 a Day*, wherein the authors document the financial life of a Bangladeshi couple named Hamid and Khadeja, who support themselves and their child on the roughly $70 a month Hamid earned as a reserve driver of a motorized rickshaw. At the close of the year in which the authors followed Hamid and Khadeja, the couple had the following balance sheet:

Hamid and Khadeja's Closing Balance Sheet, November 2000

Financial assets	$174.80	Financial liabilities	$223.34
Microfinance savings account	16.80	Microfinance loan account	153.34
Savings with a moneyguard	8.00	Private interest-free loan	14.00
Wage advance	10.00		
Home savings	2.00	Savings held for others	20.00
Life insurance	76.00	Shopkeeper credit	16.00
Remittances to the home village	>30.00	Rent arrears	10.00
Loans out	40.00		
Cash in hand	2.00		
		Financial net worth	−$48.54

Note: U.S.$ converted from Bangladeshi takas at $1 = 50 takas, market rate.

There are assets totaling $174.80, including $16.80 in a microfinance savings account, $8 in savings with a "moneyguard" (someone holding cash for safekeeping, in this case Hamid's employer), $2 in savings at home in case of day-to-day shortfalls, $76 in a life insurance savings policy, $30 in remittances to their home village, $40 loaned to a relative, and $2 cash in hand; and liabilities totaling $223.34, including a $153.34 microfinance loan, $14 in private interest-free loans from family, neighbors, and Hamid's neighbor, $20 that the couple money guarded for two neighbors who wanted to "keep their money safe from their more spendthrift husbands and sons," $16 in credit from a shopkeeper, and $10 in rent arrears. On top of that, there are the small quantities of rice, lentils, and salt that Khadeja either borrowed or lent in a crude kitchen she shared with seven other wives, an informal balance sheet that she and those women kept in their heads for the sake of long-term fairness. Every one of those debits and credits had some strategic and material value for the couple, and although their net worth was negative, their debt service was quite manageable. Likewise, critics making the poor-must-behave-rationally argument seem to privilege formal education and literacy over intelligence and street smarts and decisions made from pure self-interest over decisions based on social status and social connections. It turns out that rational is a local phenomenon.

Is it irrational to save three months' salary and on occasion go without food to be able to afford a basic Nokia-branded mobile phone? What if it's used to enable a business? Or play games? Or chat with loved ones? Or browse porn? Is spending one month's salary on a cheaper no-brand device any more rational? Just how rational is your purchase of your iPhone? That pair of Nike sneakers? Those red high heels? Who gets to define what is and isn't rational? What was the opportunity cost of your last large purchase? What is the tradeoff for you between buying your brand-name phone versus one from an unknown manufacturer? And who gets to decide what the viable opportunity costs are? Or to loop it around to the creative community—are low-income consumers obligated to choose spartan functionality over aesthetics and more superficial elements? And to loop once more, are companies obligated to make products for these markets aesthetically displeasing? Because that's where this argument is heading.

In a country where lighter skin is commonly associated with not having to work in the field, and where people aspire to work in white-collar jobs, is it rational to want to lighten your skin? And if for some consumers the answer is yes, what are the local options for doing so? How safe, reliable, and effective are they? If a multinational company aggressively markets its products by appealing to people's aspiration to have lighter skin, does it inherently make them racist? What if a local company does the same thing? What if a local company does the same thing, but makes even more outlandish claims? Most of us come to realize that these questions are far more complex than the critics would allow. The real issue: How do you find a way to listen and talk to people on the ground, whose agenda you can begin to understand, before reaching a conclusion? What do you need to do to move beyond headlines and trending topics?

Some companies, as profit-driven entities, will exploit the communities in which they work when given the opportunity, putting financial gain before everything else—just as there are countries in which government oversight is minimal and where lobbyists hold sway. But to assume that every company is that way is putting passion before logic. My assumption is that, driven by necessity and constraints, these are the most critical consumers on the planet. To create a commercially viable product or service that can meet their needs at a price point they are willing to pay is quite simply a remarkable achievement, especially considering how nuanced local alternatives can be. Our judgment of whether those products or services are rational choices for those consumers is largely irrelevant—as irrelevant as your purchasing decisions are to them.

Understanding what drives people, users, constituents, and consumers is the first step in creating meaningful products and services and eventually creating a sustainable business, whether you do that through a formal research process, more guerrilla techniques, or simply by reflecting on your own experiences. That a single financially constrained consumer gives up some of his or her very limited income to purchase that product is quite possibly the highest accolade.

The poor can least afford to purchase poorly designed products and services, and they can least afford to invest in those that fail to deliver, but they also have the right to decide what does and does not suit their own needs. The real arrogance comes from those people who assume that the world's poor are not worthy of their attention.

Conclusion

This is the part where I'm supposed to say something about what you've learned and what you're supposed to now go do with it. But this isn't that kind of book, and I don't take you for the kind of reader who wants things handed to you on a plate. I didn't set out to teach you about how the world is, but rather to offer new perspectives that can help you bring the world into focus. The way to make the most of this book is to live a full life and, armed with a new way of looking at things, ask smarter questions along the way.

Likewise, you may be wondering how the future will play out, and what you should do about it. This isn't that kind of book either, but if you step outside into the world and choose to look through the lenses of perception provided in each chapter, you'll see that the future is far more nuanced and far less opaque than it may otherwise seem.

What will you see if you aim those lenses anywhere in particular?

You'll see that even the simplest situations and interactions are rich with meaning and ripe with opportunity. You may notice how the rituals your friend performs when he stands to leave a café speak to both his failing memory and his strategy to survive. You may look at a service, whether a gas station, hotel, or café, and think about its essence, as well as all the additional layers that complement or detract from the experience. You may watch how a new technology is being used in public, and appreciate what it might take for it to go mainstream, or to fade into oblivion. Or you could order a plate of fried chicken and take in all the cues, from what's on your plate to what's around you in the restaurant, on the street outside, and evident in the culture that tell you whether or not to trust that the chicken is safe to eat.

You'll see that the world is filled with more questions than answers. Are the orthodontic braces worn by the girl in the mall really straightening her teeth? Are her parents as well-off as she wants you to think they are? Is the reading material in your friend's bathroom placed there for him? Or for you? By whose authority are those signs placed in the public park? And who benefits from their existence?

You'll see that human behavior—interactions with friends, peers, strangers, colleagues, and customers—can be framed, decoded, and analyzed well beyond what's articulated. You may even start to enjoy the things left unsaid more than those that are expressed outright.

When a new technology comes along (and by now you know that it always comes along), you'll have a sense of what it offers in terms of long-lasting benefits that point to a permanent shift in behavior, and how much of it is novelty that will wear off, regardless of whether you're the target customer or a bystander looking on.

And when you decide to go one way or another—to shower or not to shower; to walk or to take the stairs; to let people overhear your phone call or to find a quiet corner—you'll see that each one of these is tied to an elaborate framework of doing and don't-ing.

From all these little things, all these lenses into life, you'll have the means to a greater appreciation of how the world works. You may use this knowledge to get more out of your next vacation, to develop a greater sense of "being there," which will ultimately remind you what you like and dislike about life back home. You may draw inspiration from the creative ways that people make do with the limited resources that they have. Or you may use these newfound insights to reimagine your business and bring a rich palette of ideas to bear on the challenges you and your customers face.

If you look around you'll see so much more—no longer hidden; simply in plain sight.

Appendix: The Eight Principles of Design Research

1. Optimize surface area.

Surface area refers to the sum of all touchpoints with the locale and the participants of our research. Cumulative properties of such touchpoints include both breadth and depth of research, pressure (effort dedicated in some spots more than others), layers (that is, backup plans), and texture (ethics, professionalism, formality, hustle, intensity). An optimal surface area offers easy access to data collection and both formal and informal touchpoints, finds the right blend of information and inspiration, and has enough flexibility to cope with contingencies when—inevitably—things don't go according to plan.

2. You're only as good as your local team.

Hiring a local team (ideally one local per core team member) significantly increases the quality of local interactions and effectively doubles the research ground that can be covered. The ideal local is bi- or trilingual, socially outgoing, values exposure to foreigners/outsiders, is hungry to learn, and is primarily motivated by the experience.

Bargain hard; tip well.

3. Everything flows from where you stay.

Find a home or guesthouse in or near a community that matches the research profile. Make the place feel like a home, invite the local team to join the core team, and enable formal and informal spaces for the team to come together, from debrief rooms to breakfast areas.

4. Adopt a multilayered recruiting strategy.

Take charge of setting up the most important in-field interactions: those involving your research participants. Don't leave it to a recruiting agency, except when the profile is highly specialized. Utilize the team's extended social network, including local team members', advertise on social networking sites to match all but the most obscure recruiting profiles, and provide the team with a deeper understanding of the locale prior to arrival. Learn how to snowball recruits from successful first interactions, and treat the recruiting process as constant and ongoing.

5. Put participants first.

Putting participants' well-being first in every interaction lays a strong moral foundation for collecting and positively applying data throughout the project life cycle, from the local team's willingness to tap into their networks to the delivery of the final presentation. While the rule is traditionally "client first," by putting participants first, the client ultimately comes out furthest ahead.

6. Let the data breathe.

The journey from data (pure information) to insight (how to apply that information to the problem at hand) starts in the field.

Data should be consumed fresh. Review top-line data as a team after every interaction, at least once per day, and ideally for a full day prior to returning to the studio, using your local crew. A mobile project room gives the data ample space to breathe—where scrutiny can be set aside temporarily, without piling new data onto slightly older data too much and thus obscuring it. That breathing room can help you build a more nuanced understanding of the data, become more familiar with it, and absorb it through passive exposure prior to full-on synthesis back in the studio.

7. Normal rules don't apply.

Every research project is an opportunity to create a new reality, and with it release the team from their mental constraints. Take the opportunity to demonstrate that normal rules don't apply, from challenging the team hierarchy (such as letting the lowest-ranking member sleep in the best bed while grabbing some floor space for yourself), to putting visiting clients to work, to making collective changes to the live-work space.

8. Leave time to decompress.

Immersive research can be emotionally draining—consistently long days, living in proximity with people with whom you previously had only a working relationship, all while coping with the extensive demands of the project and the new locale. Recovery time is a must. Set aside at least two days at the end of the study for team decompression, preferably somewhere memorable where team members can be pampered, reflect on what they've achieved, and mentally prepare for their return to civilian life.

A year after the study, the team may not remember much more than the camaraderie of pulling together for a shared goal and the note on which they closed the trip; make it a good one.

Notes

Introduction

4   From a business perspective, there are 7 billion: U.S. Census Bureau, Demographic Internet Staff, "International Programs, International Data Base," accessed October 15, 2012, http://1.usa .gov/1-worldpopinfo.

4   Roughly 80 percent of the world: World Bank, *World Development Indicators 2008*, 2008.

4   yet more than half the global populace: "Press Release: ITU sees 5 billion mobile subscriptions globally in 2010," http://hddn.ps /1-ITU5billion; Richard Heeks, "Beyond Subscriptions: Actual Ownership, Use and Non-Use of Mobiles in Developing Countries," *ICTs for Development*, March 22, 2009, http://hddn.ps /2-mobile-ownership.

6   At various points in history the iron skillet: Henry Petroski, *The Pencil: A History of Design and Circumstance* (New York: Knopf, 1992).

9   The program was jointly run: "Village Phone–Grameen Foundation," Grameen Foundation, accessed October 15, 2012, http:// hddn.ps/3-village-phone.

11   in fact, back in 2006 Akiki: Kimberly J. Mitchell, Sheana Bull, Julius Kiwanuka, and Michele L. Ybarra, "Cell Phone Usage Among Adolescents in Uganda: Acceptability for Relaying Health Information," *Health Education Research*, May 2, 2011.

12   As the trial progressed: Nick Hughes and Susie Lonie, "M-PESA: Mobile Money for the 'Unbanked,'" *Innovations* 2, no. 1–2 (2007): 63–81.

15   Why haven't lower-middle-class Indians embraced: Vikas Bajaj, "Tata's Nano, the People's Car That Few Want to Buy," *New York Times*, December 9, 2010, http://hddn.ps/4-nyt-nano.

Chapter 1: Crossing State (of Mind) Lines

30   At this stage, we need to begin organizing the data: "Service Design Tools: Communication Methods Supporting Design Processes," http://hddn.ps/5-servicedesigntools.

36   Casinos are especially adept: Megan Lane, "The Psychology of Super-casinos," BBC, May 25, 2006, http://hddn.ps/6-super-casinos.

36   Psychological experiments on willpower: John Tierney, "Do You Suffer from Decision Fatigue?," *New York Times*, August 17, 2011, http://hddn.ps/7-nyt-decision-fatigue.

36   Consumer psychologists tell us: "The 10 Most Addictive Sounds in the World," *Fast Company*, February 22, 2010, http://hddn.ps/8-addictive-sounds; Martin Lindstrom, *Buyology: Truth and Lies About Why We Buy* (New York: Crown Business, 2010); Paco Underhill, *Why We Buy: The Science of Shopping—Updated and Revised for the Internet, the Global Consumer, and Beyond* (New York: Simon & Schuster, 2008).

36   In Richard Thaler and Cass Sunstein's book: Richard H. Thaler

and Cass R. Sunstein, *Nudge: Improving Decisions About Health, Wealth, and Happiness* (New Haven, CT: Yale University Press, 2008).

40   they had to launch a concurrent marketing campaign: David Kestenbaum, "Japan Trades In Suits, Cuts Carbon Emission: NPR," NPR.org, October 2, 2007, http://hddn.ps/9-cool-biz; "Super Cool Biz," *Japan Times*, June 12, 2011, http://hddn .ps/10-super-cool-biz.

41   But just as mapping thresholds: Mark Granovetter, "Threshold Models of Collective Behavior," *American Journal of Sociology* 83 (1978): 1420–43.

43   Still, it illustrates the notion: Mark Granovetter and Roland Soong, "Threshold Models of Diversity: Chinese Restaurants, Residential Segregation, and the Spiral of Silence," *Sociological Methodology* 18 (1988): 69–104; Mark Granovetter and Roland Soong, "Threshold Models of Interpersonal Effects in Consumer Demand," *Journal of Economic Behavior and Organization* 7 (1986): 83–99.

45   However, military researchers have found: Alexis Madrigal, "Snorting a Brain Chemical Could Replace Sleep," *Wired*, December 28, 2007, http://hddn.ps/11-sleep-deprivation.

45   In 2009, while I was at Nokia: Jan Chipchase, "Mobile Phone Practices & the Design of Mobile Money Services for Emerging Markets," December 2009, http://hddn.ps/12-designing-mobile -money-services.

46   users could hand over cash to a merchant: Naina Khedekar, "Nokia Money—Mobile Wallet Service Launched in India," *Tech2*, December 14, 2011, http://hddn.ps/13-mobile-wallet-service.

47   On the less tangible side, psychologists: John Tierney, "The Voices in My Head Say 'Buy It!' Why Argue?," *New York Times*, January 16, 2007, http://hddn.ps/14-nyt-buy-it.

48   Every time you face a spending decision: Ran Kivetz, "Advances in Research on Mental Accounting and Reason-Based Choice," *Marketing Letters* 10, no. 3 (1999): 249–66.

48   even if you're willing to spend a penny every time: Nick Szabo, "Micropayment and Mental Transaction Costs," 2nd Berlin Internet Economics Workshop, May 1999.

48   It's also why people prefer subscriptions to piecemeal payments: Drazen Prelec and George Loewenstein, "The Red and the Black: Mental Accounting of Savings and Debt," *Marketing Science* 17, no. 1 (1998): 4–28.

Chapter 2: The Social Lives of Everyday Objects

51   was allowed to wear a completely purple toga: Judith Lynn Sebesta and Larissa Bonfante, eds., *The World of Roman Costume* (Madison: University of Wisconsin Press, 1994), p. 13.

53   In *The Presentation of Self in Everyday Life*: Erving Goffman, *The Presentation of Self in Everyday Life* (New York: Anchor Books, 1959).

53   Goffman cites a report on seamen in the 1940s: Walter M. Beattie Jr., "The Merchant Seaman," unpublished M.A. report, Department of Sociology, University of Chicago, 1950, p. 35.

54   When Vertu launched in 2002: "New Nokia Phones for Richie Rich," *Wired*, January 21, 2002, http://hddn.ps/15-vertu-launch.

54   As Hutch Hutchison, Vertu's head of design: Ian Marcouse, "The 100,000 [pounds sterling] Phone," *Business Review* (UK), September 2008.

56   The "Veblen effect": Harvey Leibenstein, "Bandwagon, Snob, and Veblen Effects in the Theory of Consumers' Demand," *Quarterly Journal of Economics* 64 (May 1950): 183–207.

56 In *The Theory of the Leisure Class*: Thorstein Veblen, *The Theory of the Leisure Class* (New York: Penguin Books, 1994).

57 However, as researchers in the Netherlands: "Status Displays: I've Got You Labelled," *Economist*, March 31, 2011, http://hddn .ps/16-status-displays.

59 In a criminological study: Jan Kornelis Dijkstra et al., "Influence and Selection Processes in Weapon Carrying During Adolescence: The Role of Status, Aggression, and Vulnerability," *Criminology* 48 (2010): 187–220.

59 In Iran, where the Islamist regime: Farnaz Fassihi, "A Craze for Pooches in Iran Dogs the Morality Police," *Wall Street Journal*, July 18, 2011, http://hddn.ps/17-wsj-iran-dogs.

59 In the United Arab Emirates: Ryan Lynch, *Dollars & Sense*, March–April 2008, 5.

59 When the Afghan government: Tahir Qadiry, "Unlucky for Afghans: Number 39," BBC, June 17, 2011, http://hddn.ps/18 -bbc-afghan-thirtynine.

61 In Kate Fox's book: Kate Fox, *Watching the English: The Hidden Rules of English Behaviour* (London: Hodder & Stoughton, 2008).

62 And traditionally in Asian cities: Raksha Arora, "Homeownership Soars in China," Gallup.com, March 1, 2005, http://hddn .ps/19-homeownership-china.

65 Smart merchandisers find ways of generating "masstige": Michael J. Silverstein and Neil Fiske, "Luxury for the Masses," *Harvard Business Review*, April 2003, http://hddn.ps/20-hbr -luxury-for-the-masses.

65 As former Apple marketing executive Steve Chazin: Steve M. Chazin, "Marketing Apple: 5 Secrets of the World's Best Marketing Machine," p. 3.

69   Here's a handy umbrella of categories: Geoffrey Miller, *Spent: Sex, Evolution, and Consumer Behavior* (New York: Viking Adult, 2009).

Chapter 3: Riding the Waves of the Past, Present, and Future

71   Of the 35 million residents: "Busiest Station," accessed October 20, 2012, http://hddn.ps/21-busiest-station.

74   In a series of investigations in the 1940s: Bryce Ryan and Neal C. Gross, "The Diffusion of Hybrid Corn in Two Iowa Communities," *Rural Sociology* 8, no. 1. (1943): 15–24.

78   what were once simply handy appendages: Amelia Hill, "Thumbs Are the New Fingers for the Game Boy Generation," *Guardian*, March 24, 2002, http://hddn.ps/22-thumb-generation.

79   In a paper called "Google Effects on Memory": Betsy Sparrow, Jenny Liu, and Daniel M. Wegner, "Google Effects on Memory: Cognitive Consequences of Having Information at Our Fingertips," *Science* 333, no. 6043 (August 5, 2011): 776–78.

80   Nigeria, like many countries in Africa: *CIA World Factbook*, Field Listing: Median Age, accessed October 20, 2012, http://hddn.ps/23-cia-median-age.

82   "future shock": Alvin Toffler, "The Future as a Way of Life," *Horizon* 7, no. 3 (1965): 3.

84   In his *Network Models of the Diffusion of Innovations*: Thomas Valente, *Network Models of the Diffusion of Innovations* (Cresskill, NJ: Hampton Press, 1995).

87   It's no surprise that pornography: Chris Morris, "Porn Industry Looks for New Money Spinners," CNBC.com, January 6, 2011, http://hddn.ps/24-porn-money.

87 or about one-third of its bigger and more reputable: Paul Bond, "Film Industry, Led by Electronic Delivery, Will Grow in Every Category Through 2015," *Hollywood Reporter*, June 14, 2011, http://hddn.ps/25-hollywood-money.

88 We were a bit surprised that the shopkeeper: "DPS MMS Scandal," *Wikipedia*, December 4, 2012, http://hddn.ps/26-dps-scandal.

89 as would a shift from an ad hoc marketplace: Jan Chipchase, "Pleasure at the Point of Sale," *Future Perfect*, http://hddn.ps/27-pleasure-at-the-point-of-sale.

90 "Amish lives are anything but anti-technological": Kevin Kelly, *What Technology Wants* (New York: Penguin, 2010).

94 Still, it's only a matter of time: "American Civil Liberties Union," http://hddn.ps/28-aclu-org; Federal Trade Commission, "Facing Facts: Best Practices for Common Uses of Facial Recognition Technologies," October 2012, http://hddn.ps/29-ftc-facial-tech; "EPIC: Face Recognition," accessed October 20, 2012, http://hddn.ps/30-epic-face-recognition.

94 On the streets of Tokyo, advertisers: Jan Chipchase, "Touch Screen Vending," *Future Perfect*, http://hddn.ps/31-touch-screen-vending.

94 Google has already developed it : Bianca Bosker, "Facial Recognition: The One Technology Google Is Holding Back," *Huffington Post*, June 1, 2011, http://hddn.ps/32-huffpo-facial-recognition.

95 whether they help people get laid, gossip: Jeffrey Stinson, "How Much Do You Make? It'd Be No Secret in Scandinavia," *USA Today*, June 18, 2008, http://hddn.ps/33-scan-salaries.

Chapter 4: You Are What You Carry

104 the presence of familiar people: Stanley Milgram, "Frozen World of the Familiar Stranger," *Psychology Today*, June 1974; Eric Paulos

and Elizabeth Goodman, "Familiar Stranger Project," http://hddn.ps/34-familiar-stranger.

105   one of the reasons why tourists: Ronald W. Glensor, Kenneth J. Peak, and United States Department of Justice, Office of Community Oriented Policing Services, *Crimes Against Tourists*, 2004, http://hddn.ps/35-crimes-against-tourists.

105   The high visibility and symbolic value: "Robbers Targeting iPhones, iPods Near Venice Beach—CBS Los Angeles." http://hddn.ps/36-venice-ipod-robbers; "Targeting iPods," *Windsor Star*, Canada.com, http://hddn.ps/37-canada-ipod-theft; Jacqui Cheng, "San Francisco Public Transit Warns About iPod Theft," *Ars Technica*, http://hddn.ps/38-sf-transit-ipod-theft; Jen Chung, "Subway Crime Down 'Cept for iPod & Cellphone Thefts," *Gothamist*, http://hddn.ps/39-subway-ipod-phone-theft.

108   When Apple released the first iPod: "#01: iPod 1G: The First Original Commercial," 2007, http://hddn.ps/40-youtube-ipod-1g-ad.

108   By 2009, that figure was up to 40,000 songs: "How Many Songs Does Each iPod, iPod mini, iPod nano, iPod touch, and iPod shuffle Hold," http://hddn.ps/41-ipod-capacity.

118   To their surprise, many officers found: Eltaf Najafizada and James Rupert, "Afghan Police Paid by Phone to Cut Graft in Anti-Taliban War," *Bloomberg*, http://hddn.ps/42-afghan-police.

118   But the range-of-distribution culture in Afghanistan: "Financial Inclusion Data: World Bank," http://hddn.ps/43-financial-inclusion.

120   Entrepreneur and author Lisa Gansky: Lisa Gansky, *The Mesh: Why the Future of Business Is Sharing* (New York: Portfolio, 2010).

120   Other networks have cropped up in recent years: "List of Tool-Lending Libraries," *Wikipedia*, http://hddn.ps/44-wiki-tool-libraries.

120   to children's toy rental services: "BabyPlays.com Online Toy Rental," http://hddn.ps/45-baby-plays.

120   a "superdistribution" model: Ryoichi Mori and Masaji Kawahara, "Superdistribution: The Concept and the Architecture," *Transactions of the IEICE* 73, no. 7 (July 1990).

Chapter 5: Calibrating Your Cultural Compass

137   "I actually felt as if I were going to perish": Michael Luo, " 'Excuse Me. May I Have Your Seat?,' " *New York Times*, September 14, 2004, http://hddn.ps/46-nyt-milgram-subway; Carol Tavris, "A Man of 1,000 Ideas: A Sketch of Stanley Milgram," *Psychology Today*, June 1974, pp. 74–75.

140   quite famously after the blaze: Andrew Jacobs, "Fire Ravages Renowned Building in Beijing," *New York Times*, February 10, 2009, http://hddn.ps/47-nyt-beijing-fire.

Chapter 6: A Matter of Trust

151   On July 8, 1849: "Arrest of the Confidence Man," *New York Herald*, July 8, 1849, reprinted in Herman Melville, *The Confidence-Man: His Masquerade*, ed. Hershel Parker (New York: Norton, 1971), p. 227.

151   Thomas McDonald, who had "loaned" Thompson: "The Inflation Calculator," http://hddn.ps/48-inflation-calc.

151   When word of this strange crime spread: Melville, *The Confidence-Man*.

152   the serpent, "more subtle than any beast of the field": Genesis 3:1.

157   Over the course of any given year: Sharon LaFraniere, "Despite Government Efforts, Tainted Food Widespread in China," *New York Times*, May 7, 2011, http://hddn.ps/49-nyt-china-tainted-food.

157 to duck meat marinated in sheep urine: "'Kitchen Exposé' Chef's Confession: Duck Meat Brined in Lamb Urine to Be Used as Lamb Meat in a Dish," *China Times,* March 16, 2009, trans. by Google Translate, http://hddn.ps/50-duck-sheep-lamb.

158 When the plate of chicken arrives: Jan Chipchase, "The Psychology of Origins," *Future Perfect,* http://hddn.ps/51-psychology -of-orgins.

159 both of which contribute to brands' market share: Arjun Chaudhuri and Morris B. Holbrook, "The Chain of Effects from Brand Trust and Brand Affect to Brand Performance: The Role of Brand Loyalty," *Journal of Marketing* 65, no. 2 (2001): 81–93.

159 According to the consulting firm Edelman's Trust Barometer index: "2011 Edelman Trust Barometer: Global & Country Insights," p. 22, http://hddn.ps/52-edelman-trust.

160 thanks to the cognitive bias known as the anchoring effect: Amos Tversky and Daniel Kahneman, "Judgment Under Uncertainty: Heuristics and Biases," *Science,* New Series, 185, no. 4157 (September 27, 1974): 1124–31.

160 long-term health problems now blamed on sugary drinks: Roni Caryn Rabin, "Avoiding Sugared Drinks Limits Weight Gain in Two Studies," *New York Times,* September 21, 2012, http://hddn .ps/53-nyt-sugary-drinks.

163 At home, the only indicator is the expiration date: Bruce Feiler, "Take Back the Trash," *New York Times,* March 4, 2011, http:// hddn.ps/54-nyt-take-back-trash.

165 In parts of the world like Uganda and Afghanistan: International Energy Agency, "Electricity Access in 2009," *World Energy Outlook 2011,* http://hddn.ps/55-iea-electricity-access.

169 Chengdu, the capital of Szechuan Province: "Chengdu, China: The City in 2010, the Sixth National Census Data Communique," accessed October 15, 2012, http://hddn.ps/56-chengdu-population.

169   "lasts for 216 hours, good for the kidney": Jan Chipchase, "The Promise: Lessons for Service Design from the Packaging of Libido Enhancers in China," *Future Perfect*, accessed December 12, 2012, http://hddn.ps/57-lessons-for-service-design.

170   And yet, according to the Organisation for Economic Co-operation and Development's latest report: Organisation for Economic Co-operation and Development, "Magnitude of Counterfeiting and Piracy of Tangible Products: An Update." November 2009.

170   from lawsuits against electronics stores: Kathrin Hille, "Microsoft Alleges Piracy in China Lawsuits," *Financial Times*, January 10, 2012, http://hddn.ps/58-ms-china-piracy-lawsuit.

170   investments in the city of Hangzhou: Aaron Back, "Microsoft Tries Carrot to Fight China Piracy," *Wall Street Journal*, May 16, 2009, http://hddn.ps/59-ms-china-carrot-piracy.

170   In 2011, CEO Steve Ballmer: Owen Fletcher and Jason Dean, "Ballmer Bares China Travails," *Wall Street Journal*, May 26, 2011, http://hddn.ps/60-wsj-china-ballmer.

173   though only 15th out of 134 nations: OECD, "Magnitude of Counterfeiting."

173   Shanzhai manufacturers were the first: David Barboza, "In China, Knockoff Cellphones Are a Hit," *New York Times*, April 28, 2009, http://hddn.ps/61-nyt-china-knockoff-phones.

173   phones with built-in electric shavers and cigarette storage compartments: Xu Lin and Erik Nilsson, "Competition Drives Create-or-Die Existence," *China Daily*, June 13, 2012, http://hddn.ps/62-shanzhai-competition.

174   Lest you think they only make handheld: Nicholas Schmidle, "Inside the Knockoff-Tennis-Shoe Factory," *New York Times Magazine*, August 19, 2010, http://hddn.ps/63-nyt-knockoff-shoe.

174   or shop for some home furnishings: Lin and Nilsson, "Competition Drives Create-or-Die Existence."

174   "Does it cut into our business?": Schmidle, "Inside the Knockoff-Tennis-Shoe Factory."

175   If it seems far-fetched, consider: Owen Duffy, "Pirate Bay Hails New Era as It Starts Sharing 3D Plans," *Guardian*, January 26, 2012, http://hddn.ps/64-pirate-bay-3d-printing.

Chapter 7: Finding the Essence

179   Don Norman, in his influential book: Donald A. Norman, *The Design of Everyday Things* (New York: Basic Books, 2002), p. 173.

179   John Maeda, the designer: John Maeda, *The Laws of Simplicity: Design, Technology, Business, Life* (Cambridge, MA: MIT Press, 2006).

182   A common workshop activity: "Lateral Thinking," accessed November 18, 2012, http://hddn.ps/65-debono-lateral.

186   Major chains like Texaco and Gulf: Tim Russell, *Fill 'Er Up! The Great American Gas Station* (Minneapolis: Voyageur Press, 2007).

187   "I'm afraid I'll set the place on fire": Valerie Reitman, "Japanese Aren't Fuel-Hardy at New Self-Serve Stations," *Los Angeles Times*, April 26, 1998, http://hddn.ps/66-lat-japan-self-serve-fuel.

187   the Japan Automobile Federation: Manabu Sasaki, "A Comedy of Errors at Nation's Self-Service Pumps," *Asahi Shimbun*, May 4, 2010, http://hddn.ps/67-japan-fuel-pump-errors.

187   As for American "pit stop" gas stations: Ronda Kaysen, "A Clean New Life for Grimy Gas Stations," *New York Times*, July 10, 2012, http://hddn.ps/68-nyt-new-life-for-stations.

188 "He doesn't want to sell much gasoline": John Kelly, "The Water-gate Exxon's Famously Expensive Gas," *Washington Post*, April 5, 2012, http://hddn.ps/69-watergate-exxon.

188 In High Falls, New York: Kaysen. "A Clean New Life for Grimy Gas Stations."

190 For instance, from 2008 to 2009: "Publication of Final Results for the Third Census of Population and Housing of 2008," trans. by Google Translate, April 14, 2010, http://hddn.ps/70-burundi-population.

190 In contrast, Canada: Consultative Group to Assist the Poor, and World Bank, *Financial Access 2010: The State of Financial Inclusion Through the Crisis* (Washington, DC: CGAP and World Bank, 2010), p. 64.

192 Before it even launched, Simple: Joseph Walker, "Tech Start-Ups Take On Banks," *Wall Street Journal*, February 23, 2012, http://hddn.ps/71-wsj-startups-vs-banks.

193 set afloat in international waters: "Seasteading: Cities on the Ocean," *Economist*, December 3, 2011, http://hddn.ps/72-seasteading.

Chapter 8: The Great Tradeoff

197 All in all it's a rich environment: Jan Chipchase, "Context, Risk & Consequences," *Future Perfect*, accessed October 12, 2012, http://hddn.ps/73-risks-and-consequences.

198 the iPhone, for instance: "Apple iPhone: Global Sales 2007–2012," accessed October 12, 2012, http://hddn.ps/74-apple-stats.

199 after it had puzzlingly begun: UNESCO, "Understandings of Literacy," *Education for All Global Monitoring Report 2006*, http://hddn.ps/75-unesco-literacy.

199   At the time, Nokia was selling: Nokia, *CR Report 2005*, p. 23, http://hddn.ps/76-nokia-csr.

206   The cost of devices is now significantly lower: "Huawei Launches World's First Affordable Smartphone with Google Called IDEOS," September 2, 2010, http://hddn.ps/77-huawei-ideos.

206   and Nokia are increasingly putting touchscreen: Brian Bennett, "Nokia Unveils Trio of Cheap Touch-screen Phones," CNET, June 6, 2012, http://hddn.ps/78-nokia-touch.

208   Apple imposing its corporate values: Heidi Blake, "Apple Accused of Censorship After Porn Disappears from iPad Book Chart," Telegraph.co.uk, July 27, 2010, http://hddn.ps/79-no-porn-on-apple.

208   Coke and Pepsi logos being painted: "Coke Paints the Himalayas Red," BBC, August 15, 2002, http://hddn.ps/80-pepsi-coke-paint.

209   Monsanto's development of sterile seeds: Paul Brown, "Monsanto Drops GM 'Terminator,'" *Guardian*, October 5, 1999, http://hddn.ps/81-monsanto-terminator.

209   the very prominent suicide rate: Joel Johnson, "1 Million Workers. 90 Million iPhones. 17 Suicides. Who's to Blame?," *Wired*, February 28, 2011, http://hddn.ps/82-the-foxconn-suicides.

209   Ericsson profiteering: "Wired for Repression," *Bloomberg*, accessed October 12, 2012, http://hddn.ps/84-wired-for-repression.

209   and accusations of racism: Aneel Karnani, "Doing Well by Doing Good: Case Study: 'Fair & Lovely' Whitening Cream," *Strategic Management Journal* 28, no. 13 (2007): 1351–57.

209   We have grown accustomed to free email: Matt Rosoff, "Google Is Studying Your Gmail Inbox So It Can Show You Better Ads," *Business Insider*, March 29, 2011, http://hddn.ps/85-google-privacy.

211   These sorts of tradeoffs are explored: Daryl Collins, Jonathan Morduch, Stuart Rutherford, and Orlanda Ruthven, *Portfolios of the Poor: How the World's Poor Live on $2 a Day* (Princeton, NJ: Princeton University Press, 2009).

212   Hamid and Khadeja's Closing Balance Sheet: Ibid., accessed at http://www.portfoliosofthepoor.com/pdf/Chapter1.pdf.

About the Authors

JAN CHIPCHASE is the executive creative director of Global Insights at frog, where he runs global research and insights practice. He has more than twenty-five patents pending, and his research has been featured in leading international media, including the *New York Times*, the BBC, the *Economist*, *National Geographic*, and *Wired*, and his blog *Future Perfect* is read in 191 countries. In 2011 *Fast Company* named him one of the one hundred most creative people in business. He is based in San Francisco and travels extensively and frequently throughout the world.

Simon Steinhardt is the associate creative director of Editorial at the digital agency JESS3. He is the former managing editor of *Swindle* magazine, and he has contributed to and edited several books on global street culture and art, including *OBEY: Supply and Demand—The Art of Shepard Fairey*, *The History of American Graffiti*, and *Art for Obama*. He is also a board member of the nonprofit Art and Remembrance. He holds a BA in psychology from the University of Maryland and lives in Los Angeles.